MASTER SCHEDULING

IN THE

21ST CENTURY

Also by Tom Wallace and Bob Stahl:

Books

Sales & Operations Planning: The How-ToHandbook, 3rd Edition

Sales and Operations Planning: The Executive's Guide

Sales & Operations Planning: The Self-Audit Workbook

Building to Customer Demand

Sales Forecasting: A New Approach

Videos:

The Executive S&OP Briefing: A Visual Introduction, by Tom Wallace

Building to Customer Demand, by Tom Wallace and Bob Stahl

Procurement in the New World of Manufacturing, by Bob Stahl

MASTER SCHEDULING
IN THE 21ST CENTURY

For Simplicity, Speed, and Success –

Up and Down the Supply Chain

Thomas F. Wallace
&
Robert A. Stahl

T. F. Wallace & Company
2003

First Printing   January, 2003
Second Printing   October, 2003
Third Printing   July, 2004: Minor terminology changes and other minor revisions
Fourth Printing   June, 2005: Minor terminology changes
Fifth Printing   April, 2007: Addition of new terminology for Sales & Operations Planning, deletion of Foreword, other minor changes
Sixth Printing   September, 2007: Minor corrections
Seventh Printing November, 2008: Changes and additions to the Master Scheduling Checklist resulting in revised page numbering, other minor corrections

International Standard Book Number (ISBN 13): 978-0-997-8877-1-6
(ISBN 10): 0997887710

Printed in the United States of America

This title and other books and videos by Tom Wallace and/or Bob Stahl may be ordered on line from:
www.tfwallace.com
T. F. Wallace & Company
513-281-0500

Also available from the APICS bookstore:
www.apics.org
800-444-2742

Bob Stahl may be contacted at:
RStahlSr@aol.com
R. A. Stahl Company
508-226-0477

TABLE OF CONTENTS

LIST OF FIGURES

DEDICATION

We dedicate this book to our friend and colleague, Chris Gray, one of the leading professionals in this field. Active over the last quarter century as an author, educator, and consultant, Chris's contributions are many and noteworthy.

He has helped us a great deal in the development of this book, and his efforts have helped to make it significantly better.

Thank you, Chris.

ACKNOWLEDGMENTS

Special thanks go to the following reviewers, who are some of the finest professionals in this field. We are very grateful for the considerable amounts of time and effort they expended on this project, and their feedback was critical in improving this book.

Cathy Budd
Global Supply Chain Manager, Industrial Chemicals
The Dow Chemical Company

Tom Heldt
Marketing Manager, Industrial Chemicals
The Dow Chemical Company

Dick Ling
President
Richard C. Ling, Inc.

Dennis Lord
Principal
Inventory Management Solutions

Dan Marrone, PhD,
Associate Professor
Farmingdale State University, NY

Bill Montgomery
President
Orange County, CA APICS Chapter

Arvil Sexton
Former VP, Manufacturing Resource Planning
Drexel Heritage Furnishings, Inc.

We also send a tip of the hat to Pat Stahl for her support and encouragement, Kathryn Wallace for page layout, David Mill for cover design, and Kim Nir for copy edit. You folks are super, and we feel most fortunate that you're around.

PREFACE: A TERMINOLOGY ISSUE

The term Sales & Operations Planning traditionally referred to a decision-making process for balancing demand and supply in *aggregate*. This is an executive-centered activity.

However, in the recent past, common usage of this term has broadened to include tools and techniques that operate at a lower, more *detailed* level, for individual products and customer orders. These are not executive-centered processes; they carry too much detail.

In this book, we use the term *Executive S&OP* to refer to the executive activity, and *Sales & Operations Planning* to refer to the overall set of processes, which includes Master Scheduling and other detailed forecasting, planning and scheduling activities.

Appendix A provides more information on the Executive S&OP process.

Chapter 1

MASTER SCHEDULING OVERVIEW

Manufacturing enterprises — companies that make things — have lots of opportunities to improve and excel. Today, unlike 30 years ago, a wide array of tools and techniques exists to help companies run better: Total Quality, Lean Manufacturing, Supply Chain Management, Enterprise Resource Planning, and so on. There are lots of opportunities for improvement, but it can be confusing trying to sort them out.

Tools for Effectiveness

A good way of looking at it is to sort out these processes into three broad categories: tools for increasing reliability, tools for reducing waste, and tools to enhance the coordination of processes and functions, both inside and outside of the company. Then we can identify which specific tools and techniques apply to which category:

Tools to increase reliability:	Total Quality Management
	Six Sigma
	Statistical Process Control
	ISO
	and others.
Tools to reduce waste and time:	Lean Manufacturing
	Just-in-Time
	Quick Changeover (SMED)
	Cellular Manufacturing
	and others.
Tools to enhance coordination:	Enterprise Resource Planning
	Executive S&OP
	Master Scheduling
	Kanban
	and others.

Now obviously there's some overlap between categories. For example, better quality processes not only increase reliability but also reduce waste. Lean Manufacturing techniques help to increase reliability along with their job of reducing waste and time.

Effective Master Scheduling processes certainly enhance coordination, as we'll see. However, they can also reduce waste by helping people make the right products at the right time, thereby avoiding unneeded inventory and obsolescence.

Figure 1-1 displays these concepts graphically.

Figure 1-1   **TOOLS FOR EFFECTIVENESS**

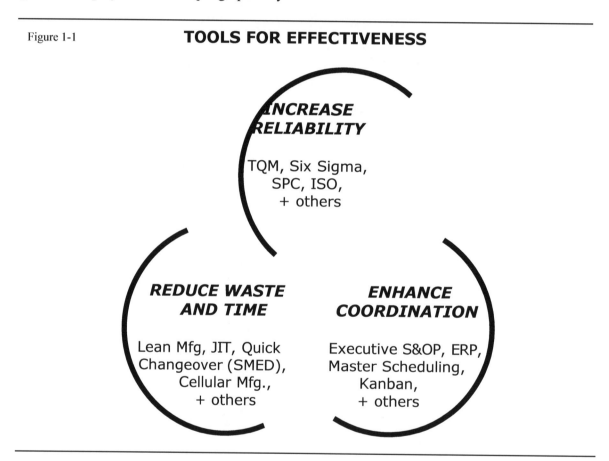

This view says that Master Scheduling[1] is primarily a tool for enhancing coordination. Okay, you might be thinking, coordinating what? The answer: two things that most of us learned about in Economics 101 — demand and supply.

---

[1] Throughout this book, we'll use the term "Master Schedule" (and "Master Scheduling"). A synonym seen in much of the literature is "Master Production Schedule," the use of which we will restrict to refer to the row on the Master Schedule grid that contains the future scheduled production.

The Four Fundamentals

One of the most important things a manufacturing enterprise can do is to get demand and supply in balance, and keep them in balance. Balancing demand and supply is essential to running a business well, and this balancing must occur at both the aggregate, *volume* level and at the detailed, *mix* level.

We've just identified four fundamentals: demand and supply, volume and mix. Let's look at the first pair.

Demand and Supply

Demand refers to the products that the organization is being asked to provide, expressed in customer orders, sales forecasts, distribution center replenishment, interplant transfers, and so on. Supply refers to the resources available to meet that demand: materials, manpower, machinery, other production capacity, suppliers and their capacity, testing, storage space, and money.

Is it a good thing to have demand and supply in balance? You bet. That's a happy, harmonious situation. How about when demand and supply are not in balance? Well, that can cause lots of problems. If demand greatly exceeds supply, bad things happen:

- Customer service suffers. The company can't ship product to its customers when they want it.

- Customer lead times stretch out as the order backlog builds. Business is lost as customers go elsewhere.

- Costs increase. Unplanned overtime goes up. Premium freight rises as incoming materials and outbound products are expedited. Purchase price variances become unfavorable, as the company pays more to get the materials it needs.

- Quality often "gets lost in the shuffle" as the company strives mightily to get product shipped. Specifications get compromised or waived. Temporary subcontracting yields a less robust product. Material from alternate suppliers often doesn't process as well.

Definitely bad news. Owing to demand exceeding supply, performance deteriorates on three fundamental attributes: cost, quality, and delivery. Business is lost, costs go up, and thus the bottom line takes a hit.

Similarly, when supply substantially exceeds demand, bad things happen:

- Profit margins get squeezed as prices are cut and discounting increases.

- Deals and promotions become more frequent.

- Inventories increase, carrying costs rise, and cash flow can become a problem.

- Production rates are cut. Volume variances become unfavorable.

- Layoffs are a possibility and morale suffers. People in the plant slow down and efficiency numbers start to drop.

Well, that's not good either. Supply exceeds demand and the company is stuck with lower margins, higher costs, a cash crunch, and the possibility of layoffs.

Now, is it always bad if demand and supply aren't in balance? No, sometimes it can be a good thing. It all depends on where the imbalance lies. For example, if projected future demand exceeds current supply, and if the company can economically add more capacity by the time it's needed, that's fine. Demand is growing; business is good. On the other hand, when changes in demand are not anticipated soon enough, that's when problems arise. Therefore, a process that can predict future imbalances soon enough to rectify them is very important. A sign of success is when an organization is focusing on imbalance problems some months into the future — and not being consumed with day-to-day crises.

The name of the game is to get demand and supply *in balance* and to keep them there. It's that simple. Balance demand and supply. Have processes in place to do it. Have early warning capabilities to alert people that they're getting out of sync. Make the corrections early, surgically, so that they can be small — as opposed to making large, radical corrections later with a meat cleaver.

Volume and Mix

The other two fundamentals are volume and mix. The differences between the two can be summed up as follows:

- Volume refers to groupings, such as product families, production resources, and the like. Mix refers to specific products, items, or customer orders.

- The volume question is "how much?"; the mix question is "which ones?".

- Volume deals with aggregate rates — of sales, production, and so on. Mix is about sequence and timing.

- Volume is the big picture; mix is the details.

Now let's bring together these four elements: demand and supply, volume and mix.

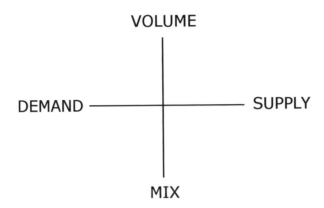

Demand and supply must be balanced at both the volume and the mix levels — or the results will be unhappy customers, layoffs, too much inventory, and on and on. Shipping product to customers with world-class reliability and speed requires that all four of these elements be well managed and controlled.

The Resource Planning Model

Figure 1-2 shows a schematic of what we call Resource Planning. If you're thinking Enterprise Resource Planning (ERP) or Manufacturing Resource Planning (MRP II) as you read those words, fine. What this represents are tools — business processes — that help people to deal with the four fundamentals: demand and supply, volume and mix. What do the people do with these tools? They make decisions. About what? Keeping demand and supply in balance.

On the diagram, we can see these four fundamentals shown with the specific business process that address each one. For example, the tool to balance demand and supply at the *volume* level is Executive S&OP, while Master Scheduling is the process used to balance demand and supply at the *mix* level. We can see that, on the demand side, Forecasting and Demand Management is a primary feeder into both Executive S&OP and Master Scheduling, as is Capacity Planning for supply.

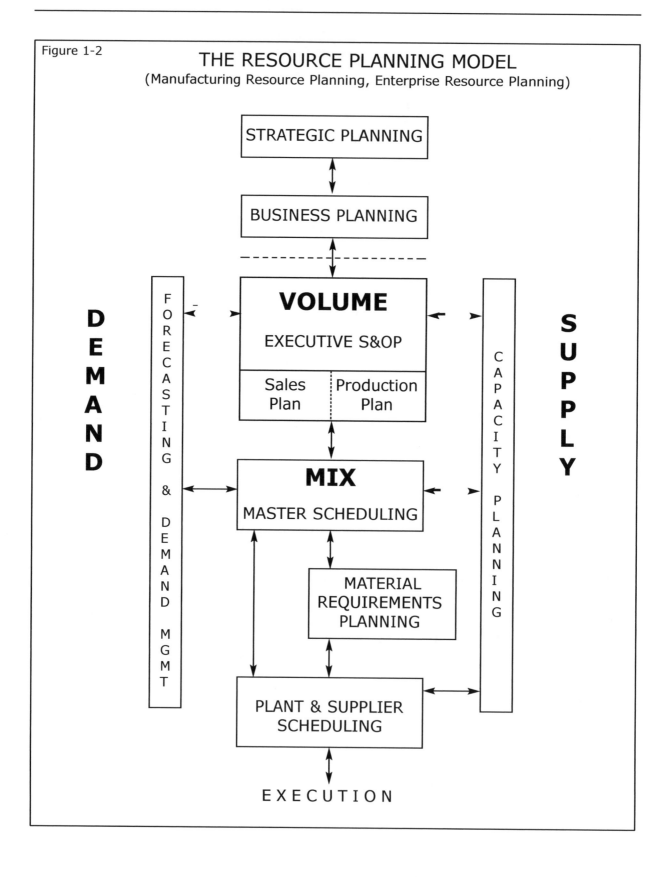

Figure 1-2

THE RESOURCE PLANNING MODEL
(Manufacturing Resource Planning, Enterprise Resource Planning)

Important attributes of this Resource Planning approach include the following.

- It consists of a series of business functions, all linked together.

- It is a "closed-loop" process. Note that the arrows go in both directions. This means that it has two-way communication: There is feedback from the execution step and the more specific planning functions back into the more general.

- It operates in both units and dollars: units for the operational aspects of running the business, dollars for the financial side. The important thing here is that the *basic numbers* are the same[2]. This leads people to call this a "single-number system" or "running the business with one set of numbers."

- It can be used as a simulator. It's possible to pose "what-if" questions to this set of tools and to receive understandable answers, in both units and dollars. For example, what if sales were to increase by 20 percent in the Western Region? Could the California plant handle the increased volumes (units) and what would it cost to do so (dollars)? Alternatively, do the plants in both Texas and Indiana have enough capacity to run this volume and what are the cost implications of producing it there and shipping it out west?

The dotted line above Executive S&OP is intended to show that Business Planning and Strategic Planning are not components of Resource Planning, but rather are primary drivers into it. Notice, however, that the line connecting Business Planning with Executive S&OP has arrows going in both directions. Sometimes the future visibility provided by Executive S&OP may lead to a decision to modify the Business Plan and perhaps the Strategic Plan.

Professor Dan Marrone of Farmingdale State University (NY) has a good way of describing ERP. Dan says that as one moves down the Resource Planning diagram, "several characteristics emerge:

1. The planning horizon (planning time frame) narrows.

2. The scope of the plans pertaining to organizational functions narrows.

3. Generalized plans are replaced by increasingly detailed, time-sensitive plans.

4. Higher level planning is typically established by higher level managers and lower level, more detailed planning is established *and* implemented by managers lower in the management hierarchy."

---

[2] Typically this data is kept in units and "translated" into dollars. For example, it's very practical to "dollarize" the inventory balances and sum them up to get the total valuation of the inventory. You can't go the other way; you can't derive the individual item balances from the aggregate dollars.

Please keep in mind: The elements contained within ERP are *business processes*, not software. There are software packages available to support ERP, and these are correctly referred to not as ERP but rather as Enterprise Software[3] (ES).

The Role and Structure of Master Scheduling

Master Scheduling is a business process designed to balance demand and supply at the detailed, mix level. Master Scheduling is primarily a decision-making process, performed by an individual called the Master Scheduler. As such, it is *people-centered*; the computer's role is to support the people in their decision-making activities.

The output from this process is the Master Production Schedule, which is the anticipated build schedule for specific products (or parts of products) and customer orders. The Master Schedule is:

- time-phased,

- extends for a number of weeks into the future, and

- is typically expressed in weekly time increments or smaller.

Referring back to Figure 1-2, we can see that Master Scheduling is driven mainly by three functions: Executive S&OP, Forecasting/Demand Management, and Capacity Planning — and that it feeds Material Requirements Planning, Supplier Scheduling, and Plant Scheduling[4]. Let's look at each one.

Input: Executive S&OP

As we saw earlier, the mission of Executive S&OP is to balance demand and supply at the aggregate, volume level. It's a monthly process, operating in both units and dollars, and it involves both executive management and middle management people. Executive S&OP has been called "top management's handle on the business" because it enables the executive group to determine, ahead of

---

[3] See Thomas F. Wallace and Michael H. Kremzar, *ERP: Making It Happen*, 2001, New York: John Wiley & Sons, and Thomas H. Davenport, *Mission Critical*, 2000, Boston MA: Harvard Business School Press.

[4] The arrows in Figure 1-2 go in both directions, indicating an interplay between the functions. However, the *primary* flow for Master Scheduling is that its inputs come from Executive S&OP, Forecasting and Demand Management, and Capacity Planning — and its outputs go into the downstream processes.

time, the desired rates of sales and production and the target levels of inventories and order backlogs — and then to manage the business proactively to hit those plans. (For more on Executive S&OP, please see Appendix A.)

Executive S&OP forms a linkage between the Business Plan (the annual financial plan, the budget) and the downstream processes of Master Scheduling, MRP, Supplier Scheduling, and Plant Scheduling. This linkage is vital. When it's absent, there is a disconnect between the Business Plan (authorized by top management and representing their commitment to the board of directors or the corporate office) and the Master Schedule, which drives activities day-to-day and week-to-week on the shipping dock, the plant floor, and the receiving dock (please see Figure 1-3).

One of the primary outputs from Executive S&OP is the Production Plan or Operations Plan. This represents the levels of production — both internally and outsourced — authorized by top management and designed to meet the forecast, inventory targets, and so on. This Production Plan, therefore, represents the "marching orders" for the Master Scheduler. S/he must insure that the sum of the individual items in the Master Schedule equals the Production Plan, within a few percentage points, plus or minus. To do so closes the loop between the Business Plan and the company's daily and weekly activities. To do otherwise results in the disconnect, with all of the potential for problems that it implies.

This brings us to our first Master Scheduling principle[5]:

> **Principle #1: The Master Schedule must be managed to closely match the volumes in the Production Plan authorized by top management in the Executive S&OP process.**

Before we leave this topic, let's pose a question: What if your company is not doing Executive S&OP, and there are no prospects for that happening soon? What should you do? Well, even though the company isn't doing Executive S&OP, it does develop a Production Plan. It has to, at least once per year, in the annual budgeting cycle. Start with that. Update it as you go through the year. So, when we mention Executive S&OP throughout the book, recognize that you don't have that yet, but you're doing the best you can.

---

[5] As you go through the book, you'll see more of these principles, which are recapped in the Epilogue.

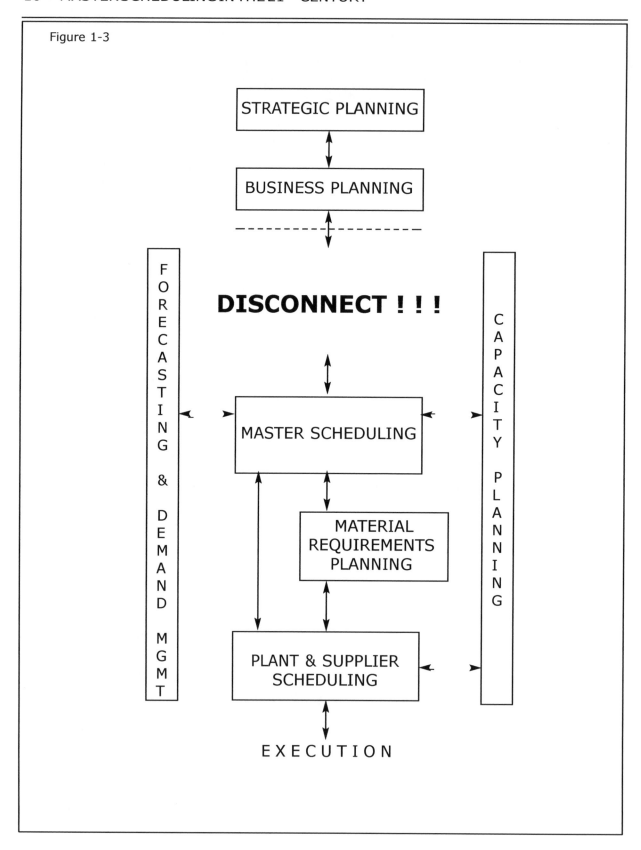

Figure 1-3

Input: Forecasting and Demand Management

Demand, of course, is a primary input to Master Scheduling, and it's expressed in a variety of forms:

Customer orders

Customer schedules

Customer commitments

Quotes to customers

Sales forecasts

Promotions

Distribution center replenishment

Samples

Intra-company demand: plant-to-plant,
family-to-family, division-to-division,
and so forth.

In order for Master Scheduling to do its job well, it must have visibility into all of these types of demands. A Master Schedule with less than 100 percent of all demands will miss something, and that means that some items will probably not be built on time. This will often create a difficult situation, with scrambling, expediting, disruptions to production and/or purchasing, and disappointed customers — either external customers, or internal, or both.

Here's our next principle:

Principle #2: The Master Schedule must have visibility into all known demands, from both the external customers and also the internal customers.

Demand Management is the function that insures that all of these demands are in the formal business system and visible to the Master Scheduler. In many companies, the position of Demand Manager has been created to address this and other related issues. For more on this, please see Appendix C.

There's a bit of a paradox here: While it's true that these demands are vital inputs to Master Scheduling, it's also the case that Master Scheduling has a key role in the Demand Management function. For example, the promising of customer orders should happen in the Master Schedule — although normally not by the Master Scheduler but rather by the people in Customer Order Entry. The techniques known as Available-to-Promise and Capable-to-Promise have proven to be powerful tools in promising customer orders with high degrees of validity. More on these in Chapter 5.

Input: Capacity Planning — Validating the MPS

The objective of Master Scheduling is to balance demand and supply at the mix level, and it's Capacity Planning that addresses the supply side of the picture. It entails "translating" schedules for products and components into workload in order to identify future problems. There's an old maxim: You can't put ten pounds of potatoes in a five pound bag, and that's the reason why Capacity Planning exists. It serves as a check to determine whether the schedule is "producible" — whether there's enough capacity to do it in the time available.

Typically the Master Schedule is expressed in units, pounds, gallons, and so forth — as in "400 units of Product 13579 in Week 4" — and the capacity plans are stated in hours by producing resource. An example might be "2,000 standard hours of workload in Department B in Week 4." This would include the workload for Product 13579 plus all of the other products that are processed in Department B.

Let's say that Department B has the capacity to produce 1,000 standard hours of workload per week. But, in our example, the Master Schedule is generating a workload of 2,000 hours — and that qualifies as ten pounds in a five pound bag. Thus the Master Schedule, as it now stands, cannot be produced unless some changes are made. Possibilities include:

- Increase the capacity in Department B to 2000 standard hours of workload per week.

- Assign some of the work in Week 4 to another resource, say Department D or possibly an outside processor.

- Change the Master Schedule so that some of the production scheduled for Week 4 is made in a different week.

- All, or several, of the above.

Master Scheduling without Capacity Planning is like trying to fly a plane with only one wing: It'll crash. When the Capacity Planning process is not done, then the Master Schedule quickly loses validity and believability. The people in the plant quickly learn that the schedules really can't be made, and thus they're meaningless. In cases like this, frequently the plant will make whatever it can, without a clear view of what the customers are really asking for. The result is frustration, finger pointing, massive expediting, inefficiencies, and — last, but certainly not least — late shipments and unhappy customers.

With a good Capacity Planning process — and the discipline not to change the MPS for trivial reasons — the Master Schedule can be kept valid; it represents a plan that is producible, that the plants can buy into, and that helps to get the product to the customers when they're asking for it. Don't leave home without it.

We'll look at Capacity Planning in much more detail in Chapter 6.

Outputs from Master Scheduling

Master Scheduling impacts a number of functions. Let's look briefly at each one, and while we're doing that, you may want to refer back to Figure 1-2, the Resource Planning Model, on page 6.

- **Demand Management**. The Master Schedule is the source of customer order promising and thus there's a strong connection between it and the Demand Management function. The inventory levels, future production, and existing commitments to customers contained in the Master Schedule show the people in Customer Order Entry the feasibility of promising incoming orders for specific products, quantities, and ship dates.

- **Material Requirements Planning**. The start dates for producing products, as specified in the Master Schedule, become "need dates" for the components and raw materials required to make the products. MRP calculates when more of these items will be needed, and how much — and then alerts the appropriate people.

- **Plant Scheduling**. The Master Schedule is typically expressed in daily or weekly time periods, and specifies when products need to be started and completed. In most plants, more detail is needed: what time of day — or what shift — to start various jobs, what to run in what sequence, when to take changeovers, what jobs to run on which machines, and so forth. This is known by several interchangeable terms — Plant Schedule, the Finishing Schedule, or the Final Assembly Schedule — and it shows a greater level of detail than the Master Schedule.

- **Supplier Scheduling**. The Supplier Scheduling process represents a departure from the traditional approach of preparing purchase requisitions, purchase orders, change orders, and so on. It involves providing the suppliers with time-phased schedules of what will be needed and when.[6]

- **Financial Planning**. Master Scheduling uses data in units — each, thousands, gallons, liters, pounds, whatever. As we'll see, it needs lots of data: forecasts, customer orders, inventory balances, inventory projections, production schedules, and more. Remember, as we saw earlier, it's possible to translate these operational numbers into financial terms, to be used for financial planning. This can yield very solid dollarized projections of future shipments, finished goods inventory levels, production volumes, and much more.

We'll have a lot more to say on each of these topics in later chapters.

Supply Chain Management and the Master Schedule

The question arises: What is the role of Master Scheduling in Supply Chain Management? Is it major, minor, or non-existent? Answer: *major*. Master Scheduling helps to blur the boundaries between customers and suppliers; it enhances the cross-boundary collaboration inherent in Supply Chain Management.

The Master Schedule sits *at the heart* of the Supply Chain. As shown in Figure 1-4, it reaches upward and touches the customers; it reaches downward and touches the suppliers. Master Scheduling is not an "inside-only" activity, coordinating the plants and not much else. Rather, it is central to communicating across company boundaries.

We'll be touching the Supply Chain base frequently as we move through the book.

---

[6] For purchased components and materials, the direct input into Supplier Scheduling is MRP (thus only indirectly from the Master Schedule). However, for purchased *finished products*, Supplier Scheduling gets its input directly from the Master Schedule, in much the same way as the Plant Scheduling function.

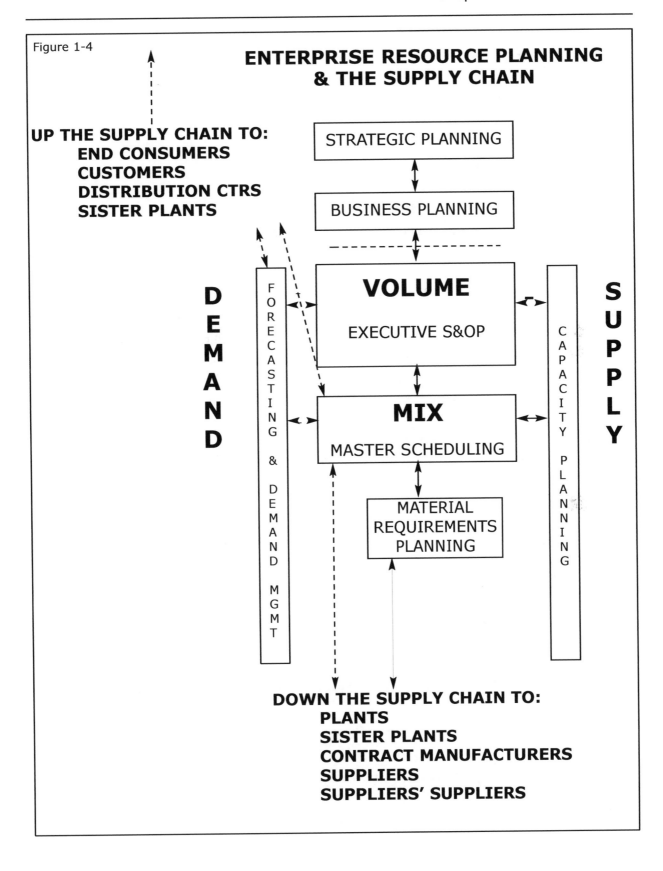

Figure 1-4

ENTERPRISE RESOURCE PLANNING & THE SUPPLY CHAIN

Lean Manufacturing and the Master Schedule

Managing the Supply Chain is getting simpler. Isn't that good news!? And doesn't it sound contradictory? The world seems to be getting more complicated, what with speedy communications, very high technology, and the rest. How can it be that this part of the world is going in the opposite direction? To get at the answer, we'll need to look back into history.

The process of managing the Supply Chain has evolved steadily over the last quarter century. This is because both the purchasing/manufacturing/logistics environment and the tools to manage that environment have changed significantly.

These changes have been brought about in large measure by developments in the competitive environment. Until the mid-1960s, our economy was largely based on a supply driven mindset: Produce as much as you can, as fast as you can, and worry about selling it later. Not much attention was given to reliable manufacturing processes, high quality, or short lead times. The manufacturing climate — with its emphasis on mass production — involved long production runs, infrequent changeovers, and frenzied activity at the end of each month to hit the monthly shipping target.

Thankfully, most companies don't do it that way anymore, due mostly to the wonderful methodology called Lean Manufacturing (and its predecessor, Just-in-Time). Lean Manufacturing says:

- simplify the environment,

- eliminate non-value-adding activities,

- create flow[7],

- make just what you need, and

- reduce lead times.

These approaches, coupled with today's very effective quality enhancement tools, have resulted in not just an evolution but a revolution in the manufacturing world.

However, there's a problem here: Master Scheduling was developed prior to the onset of Just-in-Time, Lean Manufacturing, and Total Quality. Therefore, it had to deal with the inherent complexity

---

[7] This refers to in-line, flow processes as opposed to the intermittent, start-stop-and-wait approach.

in the old style manufacturing world. Some parts of Master Scheduling simply aren't necessary in the lean, simplified operations that exist in many companies today.

In Figure 1-5, we trace this evolution. In the old days — the "Dark Ages" of the 1960s and earlier — there was a *gap*: we had complex environments but no good tools with which to coordinate them. (It's a wonder anything ever got shipped.)

Figure 1-5

SIMPLIFICATION OF THE OPERATING ENVIRONMENT AND COORDINATION TOOLS

Time	Operating Environment	Master Scheduling and Other Coordination Tools	Results
1960s	Complex	• Informal — launch & expedite	• Mediocre
	Complex	• Effective but necessarily complex	• Good
	Simplified	• Effective but <u>un</u>necessarily complex	• Very Good
	Simplified	• Simplified	• Excellent
Today/Future	Agile/High Response	• Very simplified	• Outstanding

The second stage in this evolution shows the development of the coordination tools, including Master Scheduling, with a substantial improvement in results. Next, the third stage was the simplification of the operating environment in many companies, *but,* most of them did not change how they did Master Scheduling. This is the *second gap*: Master Scheduling often was more complex and full-blown than the environment required.

As Master Scheduling became more streamlined to mirror the operating environment, the gaps went away. Very good things began to happen. Today most companies don't experience the first gap: complex environment and poor tools. But many companies do experience the second gap — the complex tools they have are more than what's needed in the simplified environment they've created.

How does this come about? Several factors play a part in it:

- Software suppliers are under substantial pressure to include in their products very high degrees of functionality. All the bells and whistles, so to speak, are in most of the packages — and many of them are overkill.

- Companies develop a kind of "technological imperative" mindset when installing the software: "These features are in the software; therefore we must use them." Thus they select features in the software that they don't need. Tom Heldt, who is in Industrial Marketing with Dow Chemical, says it succinctly: "Complex software can screw up a simple concept like Master Scheduling."

This second gap can put a company at a competitive disadvantage, much as did the first gap. This evolution is shown in Figure 1-6. A company may be at any point along the continuum, and maintain a highly competitive posture. It depends on where the competition is. All companies should be moving to the right, though, in both environment and in appropriate tools. A serious problem occurs when there is a gap of either type, tools that are either functionally incomplete or overly complex.

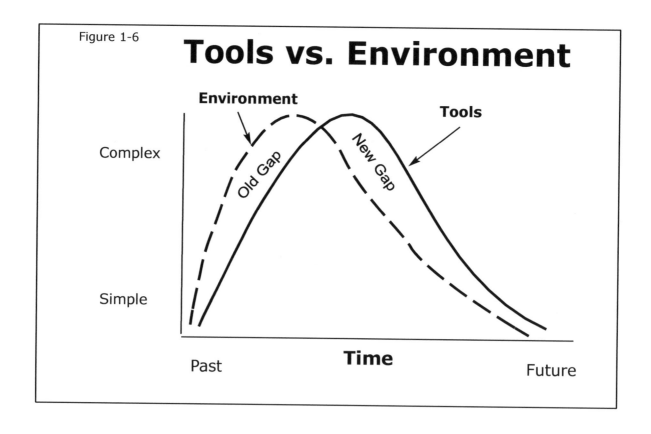

Figure 1-6

Tools vs. Environment

We've written this book with the above mentioned circumstances in mind. We'll first discuss the basics and fundamentals that must be present, regardless of how they're applied. At times we'll focus on the adaptation of these tools to a complex environment, and at other times to their use in a simple environment.

Our intent here is to help you recognize whether you have a gap and if so, which kind it is. Once you eliminate that gap, you'll get better and better at running your business. All of which leads us to:

> **Principle #3: As the operational environment becomes leaner and simpler, the way in which Master Scheduling is used should become simpler also.**

Coming up in the next chapter is a discussion of the most important people in the Master Scheduling arena — the customers.

Chapter 2

WHERE DO YOU MEET THE CUSTOMER?

Let's direct our thinking toward the top of the supply chain, the customers. The question "Where do you meet the customer?" has a very specific meaning. It refers to that point in the process where the customer order is received. This is an important issue for a variety of reasons, one being its direct impact on how Master Scheduling is done.

Order Fulfillment Strategies

Some companies produce their products in anticipation of getting orders. Others don't even start producing until after they have the customer order firmly in hand. Still others produce the product partially, hold the finished components until they receive the customer order, and then finish the product and ship it.

Which approach is best? Well, it depends on a number of things: the nature of the product, industry standards for order fulfillment time, the company's manufacturing processes, the company's competitive situation, and others. Furthermore, it's not unusual for a company to employ different order fulfillment strategies for different parts of its product line. Let's look at some examples of each. In Figure 2-1, these strategies are shown graphically.

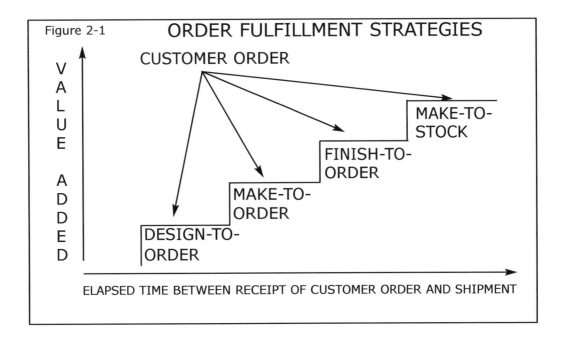

Make-to-Stock

Company S makes pharmaceuticals. They produce and package the products based on a sales forecast. They put the products into the finished goods inventory, awaiting customer orders. In the jargon of the trade, this approach is called *make-to-stock*. Many companies making consumer products — food, appliances, beverages, candy, hardware, and the like – do it this way.

Finish-to-Order

Company F looks a lot like Dell Computer. It makes personal computers in several different series: desktops, laptops, ultra-lights. Each series offers the customer a choice of processors, RAM, hard drives, and so on. The computers are put together based on the customer order. Here's the difference between this method and the make-to-order or design-to-order approach: All of the components, modules, and options for the computers are in stock *before* the customer order arrives. The computer is assembled based on the customer order, using standard components. We call this approach *finish-to-order*.

Dell Computer calls it build-to-order, which we think is a misnomer. Dell doesn't really "build" to order; most of the "building" is done prior to receipt of the customer order: Microprocessor, mother-board, hard drive, case, keyboard, screen, and so on are all made before the customer ever picks up the phone or logs onto Dell's Web site. What remains to be done after order receipt is to assemble the specified options together with the standard items, and then package and ship.

Automobile manufacturing happens in much the same way. Virtually every car that rolls down an assembly line is sold either to an end customer, to a dealer for stock, or to the manufacturer's Sales department. The parts are all there (hopefully) at the line; what remains is to bolt 'em together[1].

A related term is *assemble-to-order*. We prefer finish-to-order because it is broader and more inclusive; assemble-to-order carries with it the connotation of piece-part, fabrication-and-assembly type of manufacturing. Finish-to-order applies to those kinds of manufacturing processes, as well as companies making chemicals, food, packaging materials, toilet articles, and so forth.

Make-to-Order

Company O makes industrial machines, which are sold to other manufacturers to use in producing their products. These machines are tailored to the customer's specific production needs, quality

---

[1] We should point out that sometimes the final configuration of cars is done at the dealerships: sunroofs, tires and wheels, interior trim changes, and so forth. This reflects the principle of postponement, which we'll talk about shortly.

requirements, operating environment, and so forth. In this case, a make-to-stock strategy won't work, because it's impossible to forecast and schedule production by end item. Rather, Company O doesn't start to build the product until after the customer order is received, and this is called *make-to-order*.

Aircraft manufacturers are make-to-order. The product, a Boeing 767 for example, is essentially designed: a fuselage, two engines, two wings, and a tail section. You can't order a 767 with four engines. On the other hand, customers — the airlines — have a great deal of latitude in specifying avionics, seating configurations, galley placement, and other features.

Design-to-Order

Company D follows a variation of the make-to-order strategy called *design-to-order*. This reflects the fact that no two of Company D's products are ever exactly alike. They're even more specialized and customer-specific than Company O's make-to-order products. Company D doesn't even do the detailed design of a product until after the customer order is received. Only then does the company actually design the product. Then it makes it. Then it ships. This method is also referred to as *engineer-to-order*. We prefer design-to-order because in many companies, the people doing the designing are not engineers.

Products in this category include primary equipment for oil refineries and paper mills, spacecraft, and supercomputers.

Strategies Compared

Let's look at the pluses and minuses of each of these approaches, shown in Figure 2-2. The make-to-order and design-to-order approaches offer only one disadvantage, long order fulfillment times. However, for most industries that's a killer. In today's world, the time it takes to acquire the product is usually a critical factor in the purchasing decision.

One of the things attacked by Lean Manufacturing is long lead times, both in the "inside factories" and the "outside factories" — the suppliers. Lead times of 10 or 20 or 30 weeks don't cut it anymore in many parts of the industrial world. However, in some industries, the size and complexity of the products mandate that one of these approaches be followed. To do otherwise could put the company at risk of enormous obsolescence or rework costs.

Figure 2-2

COMPARISON OF ORDER FULFILLMENT STRATEGIES

	Advantages	Disadvantages
Make-to-Stock	Very short order fulfillment time.	High finished goods inventory.
		Need to forecast at end item level.
		Stock-outs when forecast is wrong.
		Risk of products and components becoming obsolete.
Finish-to-Order	Short order fulfillment time.	Typically requires bills of materials to be structured differently.
	No, or very little, finished goods inventory.	Risk of components becoming obsolete.
	Forecasts in aggregate, not detail.	
	Flexibility and responsiveness.	
Make-to-Order	Lower risk of obsolescence.	Long order fulfillment time.
Design-to-Order	Very low risk of obsolescence.	Very long order fulfillment time.

Many companies today are make-to-stock, but we predict there'll be fewer of them in the future. Why? One reason is Dell Computer and the enormous success it experienced by not making computers to stock while their competitors did. People can't help but be impressed by Dell's performance: very low overall inventories, adequate customer lead times, high flexibility to phase in new models since there's no existing finished inventory to bleed off — a particularly important element in an industry where product life cycles are so short[2].

---

[2] In all fairness, we should point out that Dell's order fulfillment lead times are longer than those of their make-to-stock competitors. It can take a week or two to get a computer from Dell. You can go to a computer retailer and get an HP or an IBM right away. Of course, it might not be exactly what you want, but it may be close. And, if Retailer A doesn't have what you want, Retailer B just might.

Mike Kremzar, who spent his business career in Operations at Procter & Gamble, says it succinctly: "Inventory is evil. When something goes into inventory, only three things can happen: It can subsequently be used; it can get damaged; or it can go obsolete. One out of three — those aren't very good odds."

But there's another factor that's motivating companies to make the transition from make-to-stock to finish-to-order — product proliferation. Many companies have experienced an explosion in the number of SKUs they offer to customers. Sometimes this proliferation is triggered by customer requests, sometimes by new technology, sometimes by the struggle to capture shelf space in retail stores. Companies whose supply chain processes were created when they had 50 SKUs now find they have 20 times that number — and that places severe stresses on their operation and their ability to perform well. They need to think outside the box and to do things quite differently. This is where an approach called postponement can make a big difference.

The Importance of Postponement

Postponement, sometimes called deferral, means that the company holds off finishing the product until it knows exactly what the customer wants. Three of the four order fulfillment strategies we've discussed employ postponement: design-to-order, make-to-order, and finish-to-order. Make-to-stock does no postponement; recall that it completes the product prior to the arrival of the customer order.

Postponement is good, and many make-to-stock companies can benefit from using this concept. Here's an example.

Mini Case: A Wire-and-Cable Manufacturer. Due to a sharp proliferation of its products, Company H's cables had become available in about 100 different thicknesses and capacities — up from roughly a dozen 20 years ago. Compounding the problem was the fact that each cable came in 10 or more different lengths, and that these items were available from 20 distribution centers (DCs), located mainly in large population centers. Thus 100 cable types times 10 lengths times 20 DCs equals 20,000 stockkeeping units (SKUs).

Individual SKU volumes at the DCs were low, which made for a difficult forecasting job, which in turn resulted in many stockouts and, at the same time, high inventories relative to sales — the worst of all possible combinations.

In an attempt to improve the situation, the company tried centralizing the stock of low-volume products at its primary warehouse in Pennsylvania. This helped the inventory and stockout situation, but did result in one rather serious problem: The customers hated it, particularly the big customers in the big cities who had become accustomed to picking up items they needed quickly for their current jobs. They let the company know of their unhappiness and, over time, most of the low volume items crept back into the DCs. Things were about as bad as before, if not worse, because some of the unhappy customers had taken their business elsewhere.

Company H's solution: postponement. Defer cutting the cable to length until after they knew what the customers wanted. They asked themselves the following questions:

- Is it necessary to do all of the value-added work on the products *in the plants*?

- What if we let the distribution centers handle the length issue? The plants could ship bulk cable — on large reels — to the DCs, where they could cut and pack to customer order.

- Could the DCs cut to length and package in a sufficiently short time? Yes, provided they're equipped to do so. The cutting and packaging operations will, in effect, be transferred from the plants to the DCs

- Could the DCs handle that? Certainly, they said — we've got good people at our DCs and the cutting operation is not a difficult process.

- Will the logistics planning tasks — forecasting and scheduling — become easier if we go this way? Absolutely. The number of SKUs will drop from nearly 20,000 to around 2,000. The forecasts by DC will be more accurate, since we'll be dealing with larger, aggregate numbers[3]. And there'll be far fewer items to schedule—both at the Master Schedule level for the plants and also for DC replenishment.

The result: Inventories dropped a lot, customer service improved sharply, customers were happier, and the competitors were unhappy because they lost business to Company H.

---

[3] The law of large numbers states that a series of big numbers will tend to be more stable, less jumpy, less "nervous" — and thus easier to forecast than small ones. This is why the sales forecast for an entire company is usually pretty accurate while the individual item forecasts are often all over the place. This is the law of large numbers at work.

It's time for our next Master Scheduling principle:

Principle #4: Where practical, utilize the concept of postponement: Hold off adding optional features into the product until after the customer order is received. Structure your products, your production processes, and your forecasting and scheduling processes to take advantage of postponement.

Let's ask ourselves a question regarding Company H's experience: Did the data that they used to define their products and processes change as a result of postponement? Indeed. The bills of material and routings at the plants — far fewer than before — specified no cutting operation and called for packing on bulk reels. At the DCs, there appeared simple bills of material (bulk cable, connectors, and package material make up the finished product) and simple routings (cut, pack, and ship).

We bring up this last point mainly to make the case that, when operational changes are made, the basic product and process data will probably need to change also. Company H's example is relatively simple, but sometimes there's a good bit more involved. Back in Figure 2-2, we said that a finish-to-order strategy usually requires changes to the bills of material. What we were thinking of, specifically, are planning bills of materials — and we'll get into the details of those in Chapter 9.

Transitioning from Make-to-Stock to Finish-to-Order

For companies making this transition, several things need to happen. One is that they need to be aware of the concept of postponement and its ability to yield substantial benefits in customer service and inventory turnover. Another is a willingness to engage in some product redesign, should that be necessary (and it probably will).

The third element is the need to adopt some kind of planning bills of material. The traditional approach to bill of material structure typically results in a proliferation of SKUs with its attendant high inventories, low customer service, and horrendous forecasting challenges. Those are exactly the kinds of things that companies want to get away from. So, the move to planning bills will almost certainly need to happen.

The fourth element concerns what happens on the plant floor.

Speed and Agility

Customers of make-to-stock companies are accustomed to getting their orders quickly. In many industries, the norm is to ship the order within several work days. When the make-to-stock company transitions to finish-to-order, it will need to continue shipping quickly — ideally as fast as before.

But the product's not completed before the customer order arrives. This means that it needs to be finished, tested, packaged, and shipped *very quickly*. How can that be done?

The answer lies in Lean Manufacturing. Using the Lean approach, companies have sharply cut changeover times, created in-line cellular processes, established quality at the source, and more. This has led to dramatically reduced lead times, greatly increased quality, and sharply lower costs.

Mini Case: A Producer of Specialty Valves. Company P was faced with a severe product proliferation problem, learned about postponement, adopted planning bills of material, and so forth. But more had to happen for the finish-to-order approach work for them. Industry standards required shipment within 72 hours after receipt of order. Here's what happened:

- The product engineering people redesigned the products, not to change their functionality but rather to facilitate ease of assembly. They made the product modular. This enabled them to build the modules ahead of time, so that they'd be readily available for final assembly.

- The manufacturing engineers relocated equipment from traditional, functionally-oriented departments into manufacturing cells, thereby creating flow manufacturing and cutting component lead times sharply.

- The union, working with the Human Resources department, agreed to reduce the number of job classifications from 12 to two, thereby enhancing flexibility.

- The quality control people established in-line testing processes, thus eliminating separate and time-consuming inspection steps.

- Purchasing adopted supplier partnering and supplier scheduling techniques, thereby increasing quality and reducing lead times for purchased components and materials.

The result was an astounding success story. All of the numbers went in the right direction: customer service up to near 100 percent, finished inventories near zero; total inventories down 75 percent; quality up sharply; product costs down dramatically.

What about their lead times? They're now at two days. The products they're shipping today weren't built two days ago. Orders they receive before noon are produced and shipped the next day. Afternoon orders are made tomorrow and shipped the following morning, still within the two-day window.

This is an excellent example of how the tools and approaches within Lean Manufacturing — in-line flow processes, quick changeover, flexibility, and so on — can combine with the highly effective coordination tools contained within Master Scheduling.

Transitioning from Make-to-Order to Finish-to-Order

How about companies moving to finish-to-order from the other direction, from make-to-order? Yes, that works also. Often the motivator is not so much problems with product proliferation, but rather the desire to cut lead times. A make-to-order strategy will often result in fairly long lead times and, as we said earlier, in today's world most customers don't want to wait.

Transitioning from make-to-order to finish-to-order will typically involve the following:

• Some product redesign may be necessary to create modularity at the stage immediately prior to finishing.

• The range of options may need to be narrowed. The trade-off here is a reduction in the number of choices available to the customers versus significantly shorter lead times to get the product — and frequently lower costs.[4]

• Planning bills will probably be needed, to reflect these changes and to enable effective forecasting and planning.

• Changes in the production process will almost certainly be needed to support the building and stocking of completed modules or intermediates prior to order receipt and finishing.

---

[4] Pareto can help here also. Some companies have changed how they handle their high-volume make-to-order configurations (for example, the 20 percent of possible choices which yield 80 percent of the volume). They finish these to order and ship them quickly, while the remainder are handled in the traditional way and thus take longer to get.

Doesn't this sound a lot like what has to happen in the transition from make-to-stock? Well, it is. The steps to get to finish-to-order are quite similar, regardless of the direction you're coming from.

With all that said, let's look at the next Master Scheduling principle:

Principle #5: Finish-to-order is the best order fulfillment strategy for most companies in most industries. It is more efficient and flexible than make-to-stock, and has shorter lead times than make-to-order.

What to Master Schedule

Determining which items to master schedule is part of a company's decision on where to meet the customer. Here are some possibilities:

1. Finished product (SKU) in a make-to-stock environment.

2. The parent item in a Planning Bill of Material — model, family, sub-family — in finish-to-order.

3. Also in finish-to-order, the modules or options in the Planning Bill of Material.

4. Customer orders in make-to-order and design-to-order environments. These could also be present in finish-to-order, but often the customer orders appear only in the finishing schedule in that environment.

5. Resources (departments, work centers, cells, lines) in environments where capacity is master scheduled (see Chapter 9).

6. In design-to-order, activities (design, drafting, development of process data) are sometimes master scheduled.

7. Items not in the above categories but where human control is desirable:
   - Extremely long lead time items
   - Items produced in critical resources
   - Items that are sequenced for technical reasons

Coming up next: how Master Scheduling works.

Chapter 3

THE LOGIC OF MASTER SCHEDULING

Now let's look into the inner workings of Master Scheduling and get a good understanding of how it operates. In one sense, this will be similar to taking apart an automobile engine to see how it works. We'll look at the fuel injectors, the pistons, the crankshaft, the radiator, and so on.

First, a point of clarification: The examples that follow show weekly increments, because that approach is the easiest to understand. Many companies, including those who've adopted Lean Manufacturing, will express the near-term portion of their Master Schedule in daily increments. We'll see an example of that later in this chapter.

Time Phasing

At the World Wide Widget Company, sales forecasting is done in monthly increments: a forecast for April, one for May, and so on. However, they recognize that a monthly time slice is simply too broad for effective scheduling. So they "chop up" the monthly forecasts into weekly increments using some agreed upon pattern for translating the months into weeks.

Within Master Scheduling, this is how the sales forecast would look for World Wide's product #24680, a make-to-stock item which has a monthly forecast of about 40 per month.

Week	1	2	3	4	5	6	7	8
Sales Forecast	10	10	10	10	10	10	10	10

Thus the future demand, projected to come in at a rate of 40 per month, is spread — time phased — over the next eight weeks. Does this mean that World Wide needs to make ten per week over the next eight weeks? Not at all. The sales forecast, which is a *gross requirement,* must be netted against supply that already exists.

Gross-to-Net

One of the purposes of Master Scheduling is to determine when more production will be needed to meet the demand. To do this, future demand must be netted against both current and future supply. Current supply is the inventory that's on hand and available; future supply is production that is already scheduled but not yet completed.

First let's look at the logic of Master Scheduling[1] and see how it factors in the existing inventory.

Week	1	2	3	4	5	6	7	8
Sales Forecast	10	10	10	10	10	10	10	10
Projected Available Balance (OHB = 34)	24	14	4	-6				

OHB refers to On-Hand Balance, which indicates that we have 34 in stock. Based on that availability, the first need for more product is in Week 4, when the projected available balance goes negative; the existing inventory will cover the demand until then.

But we're looking at only one piece of the supply picture, specifically current inventory. How about the "future inventory"? This is inventory that we don't have yet, but which is expected in the future. In other words, scheduled production.

Week	1	2	3	4	5	6	7	8
Sales Forecast	10	10	10	10	10	10	10	10
Projected Available Balance (OHB = 34)	24	14	4	30	20	10	0	?
Master Production Schedule				36				

---

[1] A historical footnote: The logic of Master Scheduling is the same as the logic of Material Requirements Planning (MRP). In fact, Master Scheduling logic was derived from MRP back in the old days, about 30 to 35 years ago.

In this display, the Master Production Schedule of 36 is shown as due to be completed in Week 4. This future inventory must enter the netting calculations or the Master Scheduling software would be recommending more production when no more is needed.

Lead Time Offset

Well, if the production in our example is due to be completed in Week 4, when does the plant need to start working on it? The answer is that it's a function of the finishing lead time for that product.

Finishing lead time is different from cumulative lead time. The finishing lead time refers to the time required to complete the item in question, given the availability of components and resources needed to make it. Cumulative lead time is the total lead time needed to acquire all of the materials and to produce all the components, sub-assemblies, and intermediates plus all of the finishing time required.

The finishing lead time for Product #24680 is one week.

Week	1	2	3	4	5	6	7	8
Sales Forecast	10	10	10	10	10	10	10	10
Projected Available Balance (OHB = 34)	24	14	4	30	20	10	0	?
Master Production Schedule — at Completion				36				
Master Production Schedule — at Start			36					

To Plants and Suppliers

Please note the 36 in Week 3, on the bottom row. This is the same order that's shown on the next line up — the completion line — 36 in Week 4. The 36 in Week 3 means that all of the components needed to make 36 of Product #24680 need to be available by the start of Week 3. This Master Production

Schedule, at its start date, is what drives requirements into all of the downstream supply chain:

- to the plants — for production of intermediates, subassemblies, manufactured components,

- to the suppliers — for providing raw materials and purchased components, and for complete products that are outsourced,

- and, in some cases, to the suppliers of the suppliers — when the formal supply chain extends downward to that level.

Order Planning

In the example above, the Master Production Schedule (MPS) for 36 is due to start in Week 3 and finish in Week 4. Okay, but several questions arise: How did that MPS get there, and what about Week 8 when the Projected Available Balance seems to go negative?

The answer to the first question — how did it get there — is that a human being put it there. That person's job title is normally Master Scheduler, and s/he is responsible for maintaining the demand and supply balance within the Master Schedule. (Chapter 10 is entirely devoted to the roles and responsibilities of the Master Scheduler, which is an important position within the company.)

The Projected Available Balance is, in effect, a critique of that demand/supply relationship. It can detect when more production is needed to meet demand, or when already-scheduled production needs to be rescheduled — moved in or out to better meet the demand pattern.

Let's look at the next display, Figure 3-1. First, please notice the header data that's been added: the product number, its lead time, and an indication that the order quantity is 40. This product may be one that's run only once per month and an order quantity (or run quantity) of 40 approximates that[2]. (Also, for clarity, we've taken out the line that shows MPSs at start date; it's not really germane to our discussion here.)

---

[2] There's a wide variety of methods used to calculate order quantities. Typically these are called "order quantity rules" or "lot sizing techniques" and they include fixed quantity (which is what we have in this example), fixed period (for example, two weeks supply), or one-for-one (plan just enough to cover the requirement in the period in question). For the details, please see Appendix D.

Figure 3-1

MASTER SCHEDULE DISPLAY — ORDER PLANNING

Product #24680   **Lead Time = 1 week**   **Order Quantity = 40**

Week	1	2	3	4	5	6	7	8
Sales Forecast	10	10	10	10	10	10	10	10
Projected Available Balance (OHB = 34)	24	14	4	30	20	10	0	30
Master Production Schedule				36				**40**

If the order quantity is 40, what about the MPS for 36 due in Week 4? The answer to this question is very important and it gets us to our next Master Scheduling principle. Let's look at it first and then discuss it.

**Principle #6: The Master Schedule must be under human
control. The computer recommends; people decide.**

For purposes of effectiveness and accountability, a human being — frequently called the Master Scheduler — must be "driving the bus." This means hands-on decision making to balance demand and supply, communicating with demand-side people in Sales & Marketing and with supply-side folks in Production and Purchasing.

The MPS in Week 4 is under the Master Scheduler's direct control; s/he can make it anything s/he wants. S/he creates firm MPSs in whatever quantity s/he deems appropriate. Perhaps in this case, the order was released for 36 because of a component being in short supply, or possibly to free up production time to make another product.

On the other hand, the computer must always obey the order quantity rule, in this example 40. The Master Scheduler has, in effect, told the computer, "Whenever you plan an MPS, plan it for 40."[3]

---

3 Or a multiple of 40, if the requirement is larger than 40. For the details, please see Appendix D.

But how do we know which orders are controlled by the human and which by the computer? The answer lies in the Planning Time Fence.

Planning Time Fence

In many companies, the Master Scheduler is called upon to manage a great many items: hundreds, and in some cases, thousands. The workload can be heavy. The Planning Time Fence is a way to let the computer take over some of the "grunt work" without diminishing the Master Scheduler's accountability for maintaining a valid set of plans and schedules.

The Planning Time Fence (PTF) is a point in time outside of which the computer is allowed to generate Master Production Schedules. It can create MPSs; it can cancel them; it can move them in or out — outside of the PTF.

Inside of the PTF, the computer has to keep hands off. This is where the Master Scheduler takes over. Let's look at our next example, Figure 3-2. We can see that the Planning Time Fence is set after Week 4. The computer can create Master Production Schedules outside of Week 4, but it cannot bring them across the PTF. MPSs created by the computer and sitting outside of the Planning Time Fence can be

Figure 3-2
MASTER SCHEDULE DISPLAY — PLANNING TIME FENCE

Product #24680   Lead Time = 1 week   Order Quantity = 40
Planning Time Fence @ Week 4

Week	1	2	3	4	PTF 5	6	7	8
Sales Forecast	10	10	10	10	10	10	10	10
Projected Available Balance (OHB = 34)	24	14	4	30	20	10	0	30
Master Production Schedule — at Completion				36F				40

thought of as *planned* Master Production Schedules; inside the PTF, they're *firm* Master Production Schedules. That's the reason we're showing the letter F alongside the 36 in Week 4; that indicates it's a firm MPS.

To sum up: *firm* Master Production Schedules are totally under the control of the Master Scheduler; their quantity and timing can be whatever s/he wants them to be. This is where judgment and knowledge of products, processes, and customers come into play. It's why it is so essential that the Master Scheduler be driving the bus. On the other hand, the computer is allowed to set up *planned* MPSs outside the Planning Time Fence, based on the rules established by the Master Scheduler.

Where to Set the Planning Time Fence

Factors that determine where the Planning Time Fence should be set include, first, *the cumulative manufacturing and purchasing lead time for the product*. This should exclude "strategically stocked material." These are typically purchased items with very long lead times, and thus are handled logistically outside of the normal planning and scheduling processes. Therefore, they should not enter into the Planning Time Fence calculation but should be referenced in the Master Scheduling Policy document (see Chapter 11).

A second factor is when a *product is "cycled" in manufacturing* — for example, run only once every three months[4]. Then the Planning Time Fence would be three months plus a factor that we'll talk about in just a moment.

As we saw, the Master Production Schedule inside the Planning Time Fence must be under the control of the Master Scheduler. This is necessary to provide the desired level of detail and to avoid changes that will adversely affect customer deliveries, capacities, suppliers, costs, and inventories.

We recommend that the PTF in the Master Schedule be set at about 25 to 50 percent greater than the lead time values identified above. For example, if the cumulative lead time is four weeks, the PTF should be set at Week 5 or 6. The PTF for the item that's campaigned every three months could likely be four months. This reduces the time pressure on the Master Scheduler to get lots of items addressed quickly because they're at or inside their cumulative lead time, calling for attention.

---

4 Some people call this "campaigned." In chemical companies, for example, a number of batches of the same product are sometimes run back-to-back in order to avoid extensive clean-up and changeover. Then the product is not produced again for some time.

The Planning Time Fence can be specified for an individual item or a group of items. For example, a product made in the U.S. plant may have a cumulative lead time of three weeks while the lead time for a very similar product outsourced from the Pacific Rim might be three months. The Planning Time Fence for these two items would be about three weeks for the former and three months for the latter. We'll have more to say on this topic in just a bit, when we talk about the planning horizon.

A secondary meaning of Planning Time Fence is software oriented: It is that point inside of which the Master Scheduling software is not allowed to plan or modify replenishment orders. This feature is important in order to keep control — and hence accountability — with the Master Scheduler.

The Demand Time Fence is a technique somewhat similar to the Planning Time Fence. We'll cover that in the next chapter, when we discuss how Master Scheduling deals with demand.

Safety Stock/Safety Time

The logic of Master Scheduling is to drive the inventory to zero. Notice how, in Figure 3-2, the Projected Available Balance goes from 20 in Week 5 to 10 and then to 0 before the MPS is created in Week 8. The logic of Master Scheduling has dropped the projected inventory to zero in Week 7.

But — what if you don't want to drive the inventory all the way down to zero? This is a make-to-stock product and it's being driven by the sales forecast, which we all know is going to be wrong. During some weeks we'll sell less than 10; some weeks more. Therefore, we would risk stockouts during the weeks we sell more than our forecasted average of 10 per week.

Alternatively, perhaps this is an outsourced finished product, whose supplier is not totally reliable with deliveries. Thus safety stock and safety time can be used to help protect against uncertainty of demand and also uncertainty of supply.

To prevent that, it's possible to tell the Master Scheduling software: Don't drive the inventory to zero; don't let the inventory drop below 5 or 8 or 15. We do that via safety stock, which companies use to reduce the number of stockouts at the cost of some additional inventory. Let's see how it works, as shown in Figure 3-3.

We've set the safety stock at 5, a half week's supply, thereby telling the computer not to let the Projected Available Balance drop below that. Well, it seems to have worked half the time. The computer moved the planned MPS in Week 8 up to Week 7, in order to prevent the balance from

Figure 3-3

MASTER SCHEDULE DISPLAY — SAFETY STOCK

Product #24680   Lead Time = 1 week   Order Quantity = 40
                  Planning Time Fence @ Week 4   **Safety Stock =   5**

				PTF				
Week	<u>1</u>	<u>2</u>	<u>3</u>	<u>4</u>	<u>5</u>	<u>6</u>	<u>7</u>	<u>8</u>
Sales Forecast	10	10	10	10	10	10	10	10
Projected Available Balance (OHB = 34)	24	14	4	30	20	10	40	30
Master Production Schedule				36F			40	

Action message: Reschedule MPS Week 4 to Week 3

dropping below 5. On the other hand, the Projected Available Balance in Week 3 is allowed to drop to 4, which seems to be a violation of our safety stock rule of no less than 5. What gives?

Well, the computer is behaving properly. Remember, we told it to keep its hands off of the MPSs inside the Planning Time Fence. It's not *allowed* to move the 36 in Week 4 into Week 3. But it can recommend that it be moved.

That's exactly what has happened. The computer detected a timing problem with the MPS in Week 4 and it's notifying the Master Scheduler. Further, it's not enough for the computer to tell us that we may have a problem; it needs to recommend a course of action to solve it. That's what the Action Message does by giving us, in this case, a recommendation to reschedule that MPS into Week 3. The Master Scheduler may or may not accept that recommendation. Many would argue that safety stock is there to be used, and when the Projected Available Balance dips into it a bit, that's okay. We agree, because stability in the Master Schedule is so important.

Many companies base their safety stock on the statistical variability of sales versus forecast, to achieve a predetermined level of product availability. For more on this, plus other aspects of safety stock and safety time, see Appendix E.

Safety Time

Safety time[5] is similar to safety stock, but has some important differences. Rather than ask the computer to keep a "floor" of stock in place at all times, which is what safety stock does, safety time tells the computer to schedule MPSs to arrive earlier.

The example in Figure 3-4, using safety time, actually turned out the same as the one with safety stock: The planned MPS that was in Week 8 has been moved in to Week 7 and the firm MPS in Week 4 should come in during Week 3. However, safety time won't always give the same results as safety stock, and many practitioners favor safety time. It can be particularly helpful with seasonal items, where a fixed quantity provides varying degrees of protection in and out of the season. Safety time, on the other hand, reflects the variable nature of the demand and gives much more uniform protection both in and out of the peak selling season.

Figure 3-4

MASTER SCHEDULE DISPLAY — SAFETY TIME

Product #24680   Lead Time = 1 week   Order Quantity = 40
                  Planning Time Fence @ Week 4   **Safety Time = 1 Week**

| | | | | PTF | | | | |
Week	1	2	3	4	5	6	7	8
Sales Forecast	10	10	10	10	10	10	10	10
Projected Available Balance (OHB = 34)	24	14	4	30	20	10	40	30
Master Production Schedule				36F			40	

Action message: Reschedule MPS Week 4 to Week 3

---

[5] Sometimes called "safety lead time."

Action Messages

Action messages, an example of which we just saw, are the computer's way of notifying the Master Scheduler of a potential problem and making a recommendation to avoid that problem. It's then up to the Master Scheduler to decide whether or not to act on the recommendation. As we said, the computer recommends; people decide.

Let's look at some other types of action messages. We have a new item to look at: Product #13579, shown in Figure 3-5.

Figure 3-5

MASTER SCHEDULE DISPLAY — ACTION MESSAGES

Product #13579 | Lead Time = 1 week | Order Quantity = 20
Planning Time Fence @ Week 3 | Safety Stock = 0

Week	1	2	3	4	5	6	7	8
Sales Forecast	12	12	12	12	12	12	12	12
Projected Available Balance (OHB = 18)	26	14	2	10	18	6	14	2
Master Production Schedule	20F			20	20		20	

(PTF is located between Week 3 and Week 4)

Action message: 1) Reschedule MPS Week 1 to Week 2
2) MPS at Planning Time Fence

Rescheduling

Let's examine the first message: a recommendation to reschedule the MPS due in Week 1 to Week 2. What's the basis for this recommendation? Well, we don't need the MPS until Week 2. We're going into Week 1 with an inventory balance of 18 to cover the Week 1 demand of 12. Without the MPS, we'd have 6 in stock at the end of that first week. So we don't need it until Week 2.

Next question: Why hasn't the computer moved the MPS out to Week 2? It's not allowed to because we've already told it, in effect: Keep your hands off of MPSs inside the Planning Time Fence — but if you see a potential problem, let us know about it. It can recommend, but it can't act. The computer recommends; human beings decide. Are you beginning to see a pattern here?

Third question: Should the Master Scheduler decide to accept this recommendation and do the reschedule? That's a definite maybe. We really don't have enough information to answer that question. Much depends on what's happening in the plant. Perhaps in Week 2 the schedule calls for a long run of a similar product and that will tie up the resources for most of that week. Completing this MPS in Week 1 might be a very good thing to do, in which case the Master Scheduler would leave the MPS where it is.

The Need to Reschedule Out

On the other hand, it's normally a good idea to reschedule out when practical. Some people question this; they say, "Why bother? Reschedule in the ones you need sooner, but don't bother about the ones you won't need until later." Wrong. Doing this results in a large number of Master Production Schedules running late — going "past due" in the jargon of the trade.

What happens is that the date on these MPSs no longer reflects when they're needed. Example: An MPS isn't needed until Week 5 but has a completion date of Week 2 because the Master Scheduler didn't reschedule it out — but did not release it for production. Week 2 comes and goes, and the MPS has not yet been completed (possibly hasn't even been started) because there are other orders that are needed sooner. That MPS and all the others in a similar situation wind up past due.

When more than a very few orders are past due in the formal Master Scheduling system, it loses its ability to help people know which jobs to do when. The dates in the Master Schedule are no longer believable. The result: the "informal system" takes over — shortage lists, hot lists, red tags on jobs, and the guy who shouts the loudest gets his stuff done first. This almost always results in massive expediting, finger pointing, and really bad customer service.

A huge disconnect develops between the formal system and the real world. Much of the data in the Master Scheduling system is simply not valid, and therefore the company will incur the following problems:

- Information on what materials are needed and when will be erroneous, but it will be passed down the supply chain to the suppliers and perhaps to their suppliers.

- Calculations of future workloads will be invalid, and the plants will soon learn to ignore them and try to figure things out on their own.

- Information going up the supply chain to the customers about product availability and future shipments will be no better. The customers won't put any more trust in the information than the plants and suppliers do.

A key component of Supply Chain Management is trust. And without trust, it will fail. Our next Master Scheduling principle follows:

Principle #7: The due dates in the Master Schedule must be valid. They must accurately reflect when production orders will be completed and when customer orders will be shipped.

We've now seen examples of the two types of action messages: a reschedule in message (in Figures 3-3 and 3-4) and a reschedule out message (in Figure 3-5).

MPS at Planning Time Fence

Reviewing Figure 3-5, we can see the second action message: MPS at Planning Time Fence. Remember, the computer is not allowed to take any action inside the Planning Time Fence, and this includes moving a planned MPS across that fence. That's the job of the Master Scheduler.

However, the computer can readily detect when an MPS should cross the fence — and so advise the Master Scheduler. Then it's the Master Scheduler's call to accept that recommendation or do something else. Here also, the computer recommends; human beings decide.

Cancel

The Cancel message is an aggravated form of a reschedule out message. What it's saying is that there's no need for this Master Production Schedule out across the entire horizon. Figure 3-6 shows an example of Product #13579 with the on-hand inventory balance increased from 18 to 180 (perhaps due to a customer return or possibly an inaccurate inventory balance).

The MPS in Week 3 is no longer needed over the entire 8 week planning horizon, and the Cancel message is the computer's way of telling us this. If the MPS were to be cancelled, there would still be 84 units in inventory at the end of Week 8.

Figure 3-6

MASTER SCHEDULE DISPLAY — CANCEL MESSAGE

Product #13579   Lead Time = 1 week   Order Quantity = 20
                    Planning Time Fence @ Week 3   Safety Stock = 0

Week		1	2	3	PTF	4	5	6	7	8
Sales Forecast		12	12	12		12	12	12	12	12
Projected Available Balance (OHB = 180)		168	156	164		152	140	128	116	104
Master Production Schedule				20F						

Action message: **Cancel MPS Week 3**

MPS Past Due

This message is important because it identifies an impossible condition. When a Master Production Schedule is past due, what it's saying is: "I'm going to be completed last week, but I'm not completed yet." Makes no sense. Therefore, good Master Schedulers have zero tolerance for past due MPSs. They can cause a lot of trouble.

On the surface, the picture shown in Figure 3-7 doesn't look too bad. Yes, the MPS is late but outside of that little detail, everything seems to be in pretty good shape, right? Wrong! We're staring a stockout in the face — this week! If that MPS doesn't get completed within the next few days, we'll be on backorder.

The logic of Master Scheduling adds the past due MPSs into the Projected Available Balance, thus masking the impending stockout. Why does it do that? Well, if it didn't, then the subsequent MPSs would not be evaluated correctly. If the past due MPS in our example were not added into the projected inventory, then the computer would recommend that the MPS in Week 4 be rescheduled in. But that's wrong. The MPS in Week 4 is timed properly (given the one week safety time), and thus any reschedule recommendation would be erroneous.

Figure 3-7

MASTER SCHEDULE DISPLAY — PAST DUE

Product #24680   Lead Time = 1 week   Order Quantity = 40
Planning Time Fence @ Week 4   Safety Time = 1 Week

Week	PAST DUE	1	2	3	4	5	6	7	8
Sales Forecast		10	10	10	10	10	10	10	10
Projected Available Balance (OHB = 4)		34	24	14	44	34	24	14	4
Master Production Schedule	40F				40F				

(PTF at Week 4)

Action message: **MPS past due**

Remember Master Scheduling principle #7: The due dates in the Master Schedule must be valid. Obviously a past due MPS contains an invalid due date, and therefore must be rectified. As soon as an MPS goes past due, the Master Scheduler must reschedule it out to one of two points in time:

1. As soon as we can (realistically) get it, if we need it now.

2. When we want it, if we don't need it right away.

For Master Schedulers, operating with zero past due MPSs should be a way of life. Valid dates are essential for Master Scheduling to work well and thus to effectively support the supply chain.

This also speaks to the need for very prompt and complete feedback from the plant floor and from the purchasing function. Consider the next Master Scheduling principle:

> **Principle #8: Silence is approval. The Master Scheduler has every right to assume that products will be completed as scheduled unless notified by Production or Purchasing that there will be a delay.**

Time Zones

Time zones are periods within which changes to the Master Schedule are managed in certain ways; they represent the realities of the operating environment. For example, in most plants, achieving a 30 percent increase in output within three days might be impossible, within three months it would be difficult and costly but attainable, and within three years a piece of cake. Time zones need to reflect these realities.

The most frequently used approach is to have three zones: a firm zone, a trading zone, and an open zone. Here's a typical arrangement, this one from World Wide Widget:

WEEK:	1 2	3 4 5	6 7 8
ZONE:	FIRM	TRADING	OPEN

FIRM ZONE In the firm zone, changes to the Master Schedule are resisted. Things in the real world are pretty well locked in during this period, and making changes — particularly on the supply side — are very difficult and can be quite expensive.

Notice we're not calling this zone "frozen," as some people do. We don't like that term, because it carries with it a connotation of rigidity. In actual practice, companies who call this zone frozen find that it can thaw and get a bit slushy when the crunch comes, usually in the form of unexpected demand.

A power tool company we're familiar with had a good way of saying it: "Any changes are negotiable, between Sales and Production. But the closer in the change, the higher the level in the organization where the decision must be made. For example, we'll stop running drills on a given line and make an emergency changeover to saws, but that's very expensive. Before we do that, we want to have senior people in the decision-making loop."

Another company, this one in the container business, had the following policy: "Any reschedule in inside their one-week firm zone must be approved by the Vice President of Manufacturing; any reschedule out by the Vice President of Sales."

These ground rules must be spelled out in the Master Scheduling Policy, an essential document, which we'll discuss in Chapter 10.

TRADING ZONE In this zone, it's relatively easy to change the schedule from, let's say, Widget A to Widget B, provided that the right materials are available. One way to think of what can happen in this zone is that the mix can vary quite a bit, but volume is fixed (with perhaps some capability for increases by means of overtime.)

OPEN ZONE Here both mix changes and, to a point, volume changes are practical. The plant can handle some reasonable degree of volume change, as well as being quite flexible on mix. Volume changes are often constrained by the Production Plan, as authorized by top management in Executive S&OP.

Some companies tie their zones to the Demand Time Fence and the Planning Time Fence. That's fine, but the zones don't have to match the fences exactly. The key issues center around how difficult or easy is it for the supply side to respond to changes. The example shown above is more or less "middle of the road." The zones in the container company we mentioned were close in; other companies making more complex products would probably have longer time zones than the one here, perhaps extending out a number of months into the future.

One last thought: Our colleague John Dougherty has a good way of looking at time zones and fences. He says that they're like the warning track in baseball. The warning track doesn't say: "don't go there," but rather "heads up . . . it's okay to go there, but be careful."

Planning Horizon

We've been looking at examples of an eight-week planning horizon. Our Master Schedule displays extend eight weeks into the future. This may surprise some of you, but we believe that for many companies, eight weeks is enough.

In Figure 3-8, we can see an example of a twelve-week horizon. The Planning Time Fence is at Week 9, and the company has added a few more weeks to the Planning Horizon to give the Master Scheduler some future visibility as to when Master Production Schedules are approaching the PTF. We believe that few companies need a horizon longer than about twelve weeks, and in most cases it should be shorter. The conventional thinking in this field says that the Master Schedule should go out a year or more into the future. We disagree. We feel that carrying that much detail that far into the future isn't necessary; it doesn't really gain you anything.

Right now, some of you might be thinking, "Wait a minute! How about medium- and long-term capacity planning? And how about giving future planning information to our suppliers?"

Good points. Here's our response, dealing first with capacity:

1. The Planning Time Fence should be set 25 to 50 percent beyond the cumulative lead time of the product. That means that within the PTF, the Master Schedule has full details on which end products, modules, and so on are going to be run and when.

2. Using that Master Schedule, we can do Rough-Cut Capacity Planning to calculate the future workload out through the Planning Time Fence. (We'll cover Rough-Cut Capacity Planning in Chapter 6.)

3. Beyond the PTF, we do Rough-Cut Capacity Planning using *the Production Plan* or *Operations Plan* in Executive S&OP. Therefore, we don't need all that longer range detail in the Master Schedule; it would serve no purpose. We can get our medium- and long-range capacity information from the Production Plan.

Figure 3-8

MASTER SCHEDULE DISPLAY

Product #24680   Lead Time = 1 week   Order Quantity = 40
                     Planning Time Fence @ Week 9

Week	PAST DUE	1	2	3	4	5	6	7	8	9	10	11	12	13
Sales Forecast		10	10	10	10	10	10	10	10	10	10	10	10	10
Projected Available Balance (OHB = 34)		24	14	4	30	20	10	0	30	20	10	0	30	20
Master Production Schedule					36F				40F				40	

Now the Production Plan is not in item detail; it's aggregated by product family. Because it's aggregated, it appears less precise. But is it really? Let's not mistake precision for validity. When individual items are scheduled far out into the future, what are the chances that that schedule will stay the same during all the weeks and months ahead? Two chances: slim and none. That schedule will move around a lot. Better to recognize that your medium- to long-range plans are approximations at best, and the picture ten months out will probably look a good bit different when it's two months out.

So what's the big deal with having that detail inside the Master Scheduling system? It doesn't sound like that much work. After all, the software will create the Master Production Schedules automatically. All you have to do is send the detailed sales forecast into the Master Schedule.

Aye, as Hamlet said, there's the rub. The detailed sales forecast can be quite erroneous when summed up; it may not even make sense. It needs to be verified, and that's done via reconciling the sum of the detailed forecasts with the aggregate forecast. Folks, that reconciliation process can be a great deal of work — and, we believe, for nothing. It seems to us that in this day and age, people are too busy to do busy work like reconciling the sum of the detailed forecast with the aggregate nine months out.

So how does one keep the Master Scheduling software from creating Master Production Schedules outside of the time fence? It's simple: Just don't send detailed sales forecasts into the Master Schedule beyond the PTF. You'll still have to reconcile the detailed forecast with the aggregate forecast *inside* the Planning Time Fence, and that's quite enough work, thank you.

The same basic approach applies to information for vendors:

1. Within the PTF, you've got all the detailed information on which products will run, when, and how many.

2. If you're operating MRP, you can show them which materials and components you'll need and when.

3. Beyond the PTF, use the technique called Rough-Cut Material Planning. This is the material analogue of Rough-Cut Capacity Planning; it calculates aggregate requirements from suppliers via the Production Plan. (We'll cover this technique in Chapter 6.)

To sum up, don't carry a lot more detail in the Master Schedule than is necessary. Take advantage of the Production Plan, which has far less data than the Master Schedule and *must* go out far into the future, typically 15 or more months.

Avoid the Suicide Quadrant[6]

In the following figures, the area in the upper right is what we call the "suicide quadrant." We call it that because that's where you can drive yourself nuts; it's where you would do detailed forecasting and planning far out into the future. We believe companies should stay out of the suicide quadrant

---

[6] This material has been adapted from our book, *Sales Forecasting: A New Approach.*

because it usually doesn't yield good results. There are better ways to get the information you need; forecasting within the suicide quadrant is a lot of work and you're too busy for that.

A few words of explanation about the following diagrams: First, the horizontal axis represents time, with the near term to the left and the far term to the right. Forecasts are less certain in the far term.

Second, the vertical axis represents the detail to be forecasted, with aggregated families of products at the low end, and end items toward the top. Forecasts with greater amounts of detail, i.e., end items, are apt to have much more forecast error.

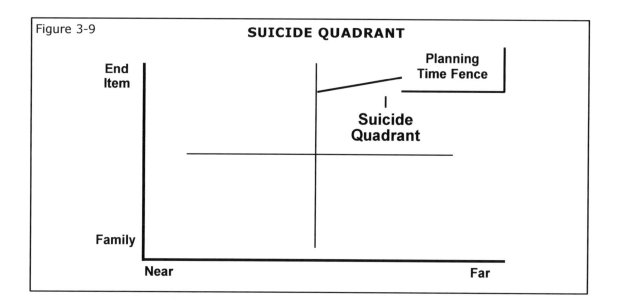

Figure 3-9 represents a forecasting and planning process far into the future at the end item level of detail. Keep in mind:

• Doing a better job of forecasting and planning in this quadrant will not result in much improvement but can be a lot of work.

• Staying in this quadrant, in today's business climate, is not a sustainable proposition for the long run.

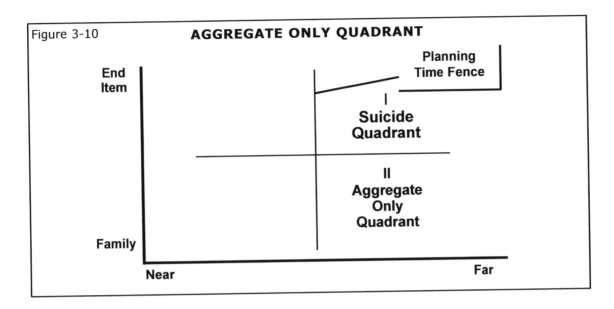

Figure 3-10 illustrates getting out of the Suicide Quadrant and moving into Quadrant II, the Aggregate Only Quadrant.

- Rough-Cut planning is used to anticipate required resources in both capacity and materials.

- Detail is needed only when moving inside the Planning Time Fence.

The next figure, 3-11, shows the Customer Schedule Quadrant. Here, information directly from the customer is used for most or all of the detail needed inside the Planning Time Fence. Three ways to arrive at the detail for this quadrant are:

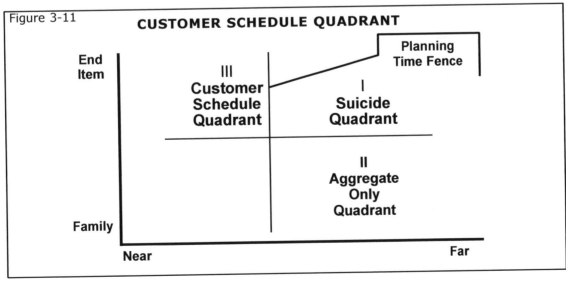

- detailed mix forecasts (by end item), or

- customer orders or schedules, or

- a combination of both.

With the e-commerce tools available, it will become easier for companies to collaborate with their customers and get schedules electronically. The challenge will continue to be to ensure that those schedules are valid and that they represent what the customer truly needs.

The Customer Schedule Quadrant essentially represents a shortening of the area inside the Planning Time Fence to a point where a company can build any product after it gets the customer order or schedule. While most companies may never achieve this objective for *all* of their products, it still should be the goal toward which a company strives.

In summary: Stay out of the Suicide Quadrant (#1). Forecast and plan at the aggregate, volume level into the future (Quadrant #2); this will sharply reduce the amount of forecasting you'll need to do. Through close collaboration with customers, obtain their schedules and translate them into schedules for yourselves (Quadrant #3); this could further reduce the need to forecast. Finally, reduce lead times

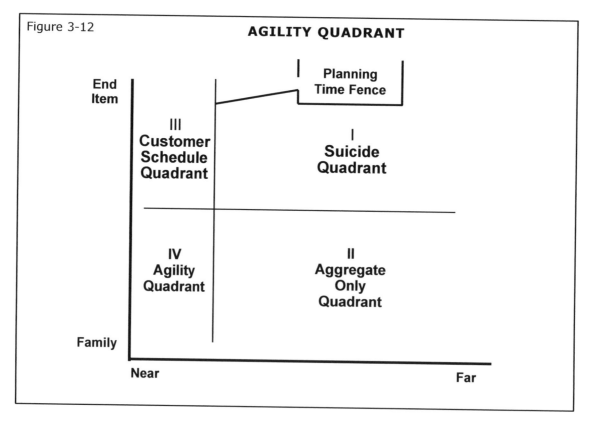

Figure 3-12

so much that you'll be able to buy and produce so quickly that the need to do detailed forecasting will go away (Quadrant #4).

Displays in Daily Increments

One last point concerns how Master Scheduling information is displayed. As we said earlier, many companies will maintain the close-in portion of their Master Schedule in daily increments. In Figure 3-13 we can see an example of that approach, which is quite similar to those displayed in weeks.

Figure 3-13

MASTER SCHEDULE DISPLAY — DAILY TIME PERIODS

Product #24680   Lead Time = 1 week   Order Quantity =   1 for 1
                  Planning Time Fence @ Week 3   Safety Stock = 2

	PAST DUE	WEEK 1 M	T	W	T	F	WEEK 2 M	T	W	T	F	WEEKS 3	4
Sales Forecast			4	8	8	8	8	8	8	8	8	40	40
Customer Orders	8	4											
Total Demand		8	8	8	8	8	8	8	8	8	8	40	40
Projected Available Balance (OHB = 2)		2	2	2	2	2	2	2	2	2	2	2	2
Master Production Schedule (MPS)		8F	8F	8F	8F	8F	8F	8F	8F	8F	8F	40F	40

Action Message: **MPS @ Time Fence**

We'll continue to display the examples in weekly increments because they're easier to learn from, but please don't take this as an indication of a preference on our part. Daily displays are becoming more common, and will continue to do so as Lean Manufacturing becomes more widely adopted.

Chapter 4

THE DEMAND SIDE: PART 1 — MANAGING THE FORECAST

Let's look up the supply chain, toward the customers.

The Master Schedule *in total*, as we said earlier, should no longer be thought of as the "Master Production Schedule." It's much broader than that. It would be no less correct to call it the "Master Demand Schedule," because the Master Schedule is equally involved with demand: sales forecasts, customer order promising, distribution center replenishment, and so forth.

The Master Schedule, therefore, "looks both ways" — up the supply chain toward the immediate customers (distributors, wholesalers, and so on) and to the end consumers. It also looks down the supply chain toward the plants and the suppliers.

In Chapter 3, our examples showed demand only in the form of sales forecasts. Now let's go a step further; let's bring customer orders into the picture.

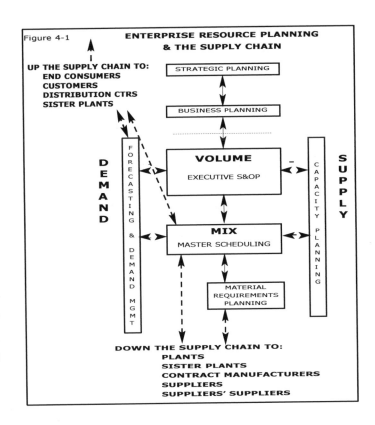

Figure 4-1

Forecast Consumption

In Figure 4-2, we see a partial Master Schedule display for Product #11223. We've added a row labeled Customer Orders. Are you ready for a quiz? What is the Projected Available Balance at the end of Week 1? Before the customer order for 7 was booked, we can safely say that the balance was 26. But what is it now?

Figure 4-2   **MASTER SCHEDULE DISPLAY — CUSTOMER ORDERS**

Product #11223   Lead Time = 1 week   Order Quantity = 25

Week	PAST DUE	1	2	3	4	5	6	7	8
Sales Forecast		10	10	10	10	10	10	10	10
Customer Orders		7							
Projected Available Balance (OHB = 36)		?							

The answer: 26. It hasn't changed. The logic of Master Scheduling assumes that the customer order is part of the sales forecast, not an addition to it. Let's look at the same item, but with a complete display of information[1] (see Figure 4-3).

Figure 4-3   **MASTER SCHEDULE DISPLAY — FORECAST CONSUMPTION**

Product #11223   Lead Time = 1 week   Order Quantity = 25
Planning Time Fence @ Week 7

Week	PAST DUE	1	2	3	4	5	6	7	PTF 8
Sales Forecast		**3**	10	10	10	10	10	10	10
Customer Orders		**7**							
Total Demand		**10**	**10**	**10**	**10**	**10**	**10**	**10**	**10**
Projected Available Balance (OHB = 36)		26	16	6	21	11	1	16	6
Master Production Schedule					25F			25F	

---

[1] Master Scheduling experts may have noticed that the Available-to-Promise row is missing. That's deliberate. In this chapter, we're concentrating on the mechanics of forecast consumption and related issues. For simplicity's sake, we'll delay introducing order promising until the next chapter.

The first thing to note is that the forecast has been reduced ("consumed" in the jargon of Master Scheduling) by 7, the amount of the customer order. Doing this has enabled the Total Demand row to contain 10 in Week 1, not 17. In other words, the Total Demand is the same as it was before the order was booked. This kept the Projected Available Balance the same as before, which is *very important.*

Here's why. Let's pretend for a moment that the forecast was not consumed by the customer order. The following would result, as shown in Figure 4-4:

Figure 4-4

ERRONEOUS MASTER SCHEDULE DISPLAY #1

Product #11223   Lead Time = 1 week   Order Quantity = 25
Planning Time Fence @ Week 7

Week	PAST DUE	1	2	3	4	5	6	7	PTF 8
Sales Forecast		10	10	10	10	10	10	10	10
Customer Orders		7							
Total Demand		17	10	10	10	10	10	10	10
Projected Available Balance (OHB = 36)		19	9	-1	14	4	-6	9	24
Master Production Schedule (MPS)					25F			25F	25

Action Message: **Reschedule MPS Week 4 to Week 3**
Reschedule MPS Week 7 to Week 6
MPS at Planning Time Fence

What a mess! The Projected Available Balance is incorrect because the forecast was not consumed properly. This bad balance caused the computer to generate two reschedule-in recommendations, neither of which is valid. Also, responding to the negative balance in Week 8, the computer set up a new MPS and told the Master Scheduler to move it across the time fence during this week.

All of the action messages in Figure 4-4 are erroneous. The correct picture for this product is shown back in Figure 4-3, which contains no action messages. Product #11223 is stable and under control.

Erroneous action messages tell people to do the wrong thing. If people accept the message and take the wrong action, things will get messed up pretty quickly. If this happens often enough, people are forced into closely scrutinizing each action message, which probably takes more time than they have, or to ignore the action messages completely and fly by the seat of their pants. In either case, Master Scheduling will be ineffective.

Action messages are important, *but they must be valid.* They're the computer's way of notifying us human beings that something's not right, that we're probably going to have a problem at some point unless we take action. Valid action messages help to keep us out of trouble. Invalid action messages are like the boy who cried "wolf!" Wolf was an invalid action message. After a time, people ignored it[2].

Back to forecast consumption. Our message here is that the forecast must be consumed correctly. If not, Master Scheduling won't work. And thus the supply chain will not be managed nearly as well as it could be. Customer service will suffer, inventories will be too high, and costs will be much higher than necessary.

Chris Gray makes an excellent point in this regard: "Even with valid forecast consumption logic, the Master Scheduler still has a challenging job and the question 'Is demand really changing?' can be a tough one to answer. One of the most important parts of the Master Scheduler's job is to not 'chase demand.' In other words, the Master Scheduler has to work hard not to jerk the schedule around because one day the demand is up, the next day down, the next day up, and on and on."

How Not to Consume the Forecast

Some people take a different approach to consuming the forecast: They use the greater of forecast or actual customer orders. How that works is shown in Figure 4-5.

---

[2] We need to distinguish between erroneous action messages and those that are trivial. Trivial action messages are often triggered by a very minor condition; examples include penetration of safety stock by one unit, or a reschedule out by one day. These are valid messages, but normally it's not necessary to act on them. Sometimes it's not even desirable to act on them. Good Master Schedulers learn to recognize trivial action messages and to disregard them.

Once again, things are messed up. The sales forecast for the first four weeks had totaled 80. However, we're now showing total demand in Weeks 1 through 4 to be 84 (20 + 24 + 20 + 20). Why? Not because of higher sales. In fact, for the first two weeks of the month, our month-to-date sales are 36, slightly *below* forecast. This is not a problem, but it's certainly not a reason to increase the forecast for the month.

By using the greater of forecast or actual sales, the Projected Available Balance goes negative in Week 4. This would cause the computer to issue recommendations to reschedule the orders due in Weeks 5 and 8. Here again, if the Master Scheduler did so, s/he would be creating instability and forcing unnecessary schedule changes that could cause "nervousness" in the process, be expensive, and be damaging to morale.

Figure 4-5   **ERRONEOUS MASTER SCHEDULE DISPLAY   #2**

Product #97531   Lead Time = 1 week   Order Quantity = 60

Week	PAST DUE	1	2	3	4	5	6	7	8
Sales Forecast		20	20	20	20	20	20	20	20
Customer Orders		12	24						
Total Demand		20	24	20	20	20	20	20	20
Projected Available Balance (OHB = 80)		60	36	16	-4	36	16	-4	36
Master Production Schedule						60F			60F

Action Message: Reschedule MPS Week 5 to Week 4
Reschedule MPS Week 6 to Week 5

This approach is one reason why so many resource planning efforts (MRP II/ERP) have not worked well. The forecast was not consumed correctly, and this caused erroneous and unstable demand data to routinely enter the Master Scheduling process. When this happens, the entire supply chain suffers. "For want of a nail, the kingdom was lost . . ."

Figure 4-6 shows how Product #97531 would look had the forecast been consumed properly.

Figure 4-6

MASTER SCHEDULE DISPLAY — CORRECT FORECAST CONSUMPTION

Product #97531   Lead Time = 1 week   Order Quantity = 60

Week	PAST DUE	1	2	3	4	5	6	7	8
Sales Forecast	4	0	20	20	20	20	20	20	
Customer Orders		12	24						
Total Demand	16	24	20	20	20	20	20	20	
Projected Available Balance (OHB = 80)	64	40	20	0	40	20	0	40	
Master Production Schedule					60F			60F	

Action Message:

Isn't this better?! The action messages have gone away because the forecast was consumed properly:

•   The orders for 12 in Week 1 consumed 12 out of the forecast, leaving 8.

•   The order for 24 in Week 2 consumed all 20 of the Week 2 forecast, but there were 4 left over.

•   Those 4 were consumed out of the Week 1 forecast, dropping the unconsumed forecast to 4.

The logic of Master Scheduling in these cases is to consume first from the prior period(s).

Now on to the next Master Scheduling principle.

Principle #9: Valid forecast consumption is essential for Master Scheduling to work properly.

When the forecast is consumed correctly, the Master Scheduler can see the most accurate representation of demand. S/he can get an early warning on changes in demand and will to be able to make a realistic assessment of action messages as things change.

Let's go back to Product #11223. When we last saw it, in Figure 4-4, we had booked orders for 7 in Week 1. Now let's say we've just received a customer order for 18 in Week 3. In Figure 4-7, we can see how the display would look after booking that order.

Figure 4-7

MASTER SCHEDULE DISPLAY — ADDITIONAL ORDER #1

Product #11223   Lead Time = 1 week   Order Quantity = 25
                     Planning Time Fence @ Week 7

Week	PAST DUE	1	2	3	4	5	6	7	PTF 8
Sales Forecast		3	2	0	10	10	10	10	10
Customer Orders		7		18					
Total Demand		10	2	18	10	10	10	10	10
Projected Available Balance (OHB = 36)		26	24	6	21	11	1	16	6
Master Production Schedule (MPS)					25F			25F	

Please notice what happened. The customer order for 18 consumed all 10 of the Week 3 forecast; it's now zero. That left 8 still unconsumed, which it got from Week 2. Two important things have occurred here:

1. Both of the customer orders are shown in the weeks when they're promised. (Again, how to promise customer orders will be covered in Chapter 5.)

2. The total demand has not changed, only its timing. During the first three weeks, before we booked any orders, the demand was 30. Now, after booking orders for 25, the total demand is still 30 during Weeks 1 through 3.

Also there's one important thing that *has not occurred*: The computer didn't generate any erroneous action messages. The MPSs in Weeks 4 and 7 are still shown as timed properly, because the forecast was consumed validly.

Some of you might be thinking: Aren't you guys playing fast and loose with the forecast? After all, you're reducing the forecast in weeks that are different from when the order is called for. Our response: no, not at all.

Let us ask you a question in return: Whoever said that this forecast of 10 per week is going to reflect exactly how the customer demand is going to come in? The forecast is for 40 per month, which got "chopped up" into weeks to enable the supply side of Master Scheduling to work properly. Please keep in mind: The forecast exists to get us "in the ballpark." It will be wrong, and the challenge is to replace — quickly and validly — the uncertainty of the forecast with the certainty of sold orders.

A day later, we get another order for Product #11223, this one for 28 in Week 4. Let's take a look at Figure 4-8.

Figure 4-8   **MASTER SCHEDULE DISPLAY — ADDITIONAL ORDER #2**

Product #11223   Lead Time = 1 week   Order Quantity = 25
                    Planning Time fence @ Week 7

Week	PAST DUE	1	2	3	4	5	6	7	PTF 8
Sales Forecast		0	0	0	0	0	7	10	10
Customer Orders		7		18	28				
Total Demand		7	0	18	28	0	7	10	10
Projected Available Balance (OHB = 36)		29	29	11	8	8	1	16	6
Master Production Schedule					25F			25F	

Action Message:

Order Detail:	Week	Qty	Customer	Order #
	1	7	Jones	13579
	3	10	Smith - LA	24680L
	3	8	Smith - NY	24680N
	4	28	National	35791

Well, this order for 28 consumed the 10 in Week 4, and then moved left and consumed the 2 in Week 2 and the 3 in Week 1. That's 15; it still had 13 to go. Since it couldn't go any farther to the left, it looked to the right. It took all 10 from Week 5 and 3 from Week 6, for a total of 28 — the amount of the order. (The recommended approach to forecast consumption says to consume first from the left. When there's no more there, consume from the right.)

One last point: Some new data has been added to Figure 4-7, in the section labeled "Order Detail." This feature, also called "pegging," gives the details of the customer orders. This can be extremely helpful — some would call it essential — to the Master Scheduler in investigating, diagnosing, and solving problems.

Demand Time Fence

Some companies find that they need to consume the forecast even if they haven't sold all of it. An example of this is a company whose make-to-order products take about four weeks to produce. Production can't be started until the customer order has been received and the complete specifications are known.

Therefore, within that first four-week period, any forecast would be invalid. They either have the customer orders in the first four weeks (in which case they produce them) or they don't have the orders and *can't* produce. What they need to do is ignore all forecasts during Weeks 1 through 4. The Demand Time Fence does just that. It eliminates the forecast during the periods inside of it, i.e., to its left. Let's check Figure 4-9.

Here we can see that the Demand Time Fence has been set at four weeks. This results in eliminating all of the forecasts inside of it. Without the Demand Time Fence, a forecast of 1 would still be present in Week 2, and the forecast row in Week 3 would show 2.

Let's shift our attention for a moment to the Master Production Schedule row. Master Production Schedules with a suffix of F (for firm — under Master Scheduler control) are still in a planning state and have not yet been released, but are driving lower level demand for components and materials.

Now note the letter R after the quantities in the first four weeks. That stands for "released." This product has a four-week lead time to produce and thus all orders in the first four weeks have been

Figure 4-9

MASTER SCHEDULE DISPLAY — DEMAND TIME FENCE

Product #11226   Lead Time = 4 weeks   Order Quantity = 1 for 1
Planning Time Fence @ Week 7
Demand Time Fence @ Week 4

Week	PAST DUE	1	2	3	4	5	6	7	8
Sales Forecast						1	7	10	10
Customer Orders		10	9	8	10	9	3		
Total Demand		10	9	8	10	10	10	10	10
Projected Available Balance (OHB = 0)		0	0	0	0	0	0	0	0
Master Production Schedule	10R	9R	8R	10R	10F	10F	10F	10	

DTF is between week 4 and 5. PTF is between week 7 and 8.

Action Message: **MPS at Planning Time Fence**

released into production, typically by the Master Scheduler[3]. These orders exist in the real world. Several points regarding order releasing in a traditional environment:

- Prior to order release, the Master Scheduler would verify that the quantity of the MPS is the amount needed. In Figure 4-9, the Master Scheduler reduced the MPSs in the second and third weeks to 9 and 8, respectively, to match the customer orders. These MPSs probably had been for quantities of 10 until they moved close in and were released.

- Also prior to order release, the Master Scheduler would perform a *component availability check.* This uses a piece of software that does a single-level bill of material explosion and verifies that there are enough components available to make the quantity of the MPS. If there are, fine; the Master Scheduler authorizes the order to be released. If not, then the Master Scheduler has a decision from among the following options:

---

[3] In some organizations, the Master Scheduler will release the MPS orders into production. In others, the Master Scheduler identifies the orders to be released and hands them off to another individual, perhaps in the Production Control group.

1. Don't release the MPS. Wait for the shortage(s) to clear.

2. Reduce the quantity of the MPS to what can be made from the existing components and release the MPS.

3. Release the MPS for the full quantity, deliberately creating a shortage but knowing that the shortage will be covered by an order due to arrive soon.

4 Release the MPS for the full quantity, authorizing a substitution for the short component(s).

Figure 4-10

ERRONEOUS MASTER SCHEDULE DISPLAY #3

Product #11226   Lead Time = 4 weeks   Order Quantity = 1 for 1
                         Planning Time Fence @ Week 6
                         Demand Time Fence @ Week 4

Week	PAST DUE	1	2	3	4	DTF 5	6	PTF 7	8
Sales Forecast			1	2		1	7	10	10
Customer Orders		10	9	8	10	9	3		
Total Demand		10	10	10	10	10	10	10	10
Projected Available Balance (OHB = 0)		0	-1	-3	-3	-3	-3	0	0
Master Production Schedule	10R	9R	8R	10R	10F	10F	13	10	

Action Message: **Reschedule MPS Week 3 to Week 2**
                                     Reschedule MPS Week 4 to Week 3
                                     Reschedule MPS Week 5 to Week 4
                                     Reschedule MPS Week 6 to Week 5
                                     Reschedule MPS Week 7 to Week 6
                                     MPS at Planning Time Fence

Back to the Demand Time Fence. It's a handy way of allowing only actual demand into that close-in period. This takes the maintenance burden off the Master Scheduler and, even more important, it reduces the possibility for erroneous action messages and, hence, human mistakes.

In our example, let's say that the Demand Time Fence was not present and that the Master Scheduler failed to zero out the unsold forecast in Weeks 2 and 3. The result is shown in Figure 4-10.

What we get is a bunch of erroneous action messages, as the logic of the system tries to cover the perceived shortages in Weeks 2 and 3. These shortages are fictitious, created by keeping forecast numbers in those weeks even though it's impossible to build them and get them shipped.

Rolling the Forecast

Are you ready for another quiz? Here goes. We have a product with a forecast of 40 per four-week period, which we chop up into 10 per week.

Week:	1	2	3	4	Total Demand
Forecast:	10	10	10	10	40

During Week 1, we sell and ship 8. At the end of Week 1, the picture looks like this.

Week:	1 Today	2	3	4	Total Demand
Forecast:		10	10	10	?
Sales:	8				

Now for the quiz: After Week 1 is over, what's the forecast for Week 2? If you said 12, you get a gold star. However, some of you may be thinking: Wait a minute. That's changing the forecast. Our response: Is it really? Let's take a closer look. If we *don't* make the software roll the quantity of 2 from Week 1 into Week 2, then the total expected demand for this product during this four-week period has become 38 (8 + 10 + 10 + 10). We have, inadvertently no doubt, *changed the forecast.*

By rolling the undersold (and oversold) portions of the forecasts into the following week, we keep the demand stream stable. One more time: The orders are not going to arrive in equal amounts each week. Nobody, least of all the folks in Sales & Marketing, is predicting that orders for exactly 10 will come in each week. See below.

Week:	1	Today 2	3	4	Total Demand
Forecast:		12	10	10	32
Sales:	8				8
					40

In Week 2, we sell 13 — and the following picture results.

Week:	1	2	Today 3	4	Total Demand
Forecast:			9	10	19
Sales:	8	13			21
					40

In Week 3 we sell 9, and in Week 4 we sell 7. After that, here's how it looks.

Week:	1	2	3	Today 4	Total Demand
Forecast:					
Sales:	8	13	9	7	37
					37

The month is over, and we've sold 37 versus a forecast of 40. But what do we do with the undersold quantity of 3? Well, we have two choices: roll it or drop it. We can roll it into the next month, in effect saying that the 3 that didn't get ordered this month were just late getting here and they'll show up next month along with the entire forecast for that month. Or, we can say that the shortfall of 3 was simply random forecast error and can safely be ignored. Next month we might sell 5 more than the forecast, and 2 less during the following month.

Most companies choose the latter course. Their systems are set to drop the oversold or undersold quantities unless a human being intervenes and manually overrides the default logic. This allows the forecaster, typically someone in Sales & Marketing, to specify those cases where the oversale or undersale was caused by timing, but not to have to worry about each and every item. Not dropping the over/undersold forecast at the end of the month has caused problems for more than a few companies.

Reconciliation — Detailed Forecast to Aggregate

Inside the Planning Time Fence, many companies require sales forecasts at the detail level: individual products, SKUs, and so forth. Remember, inside the PTF, we're operating at that level, and hence detailed forecasts are needed.

Let's say that the PTF is set after Week 8, so we have detailed forecasts through that period. Let's also say that we have aggregate forecasts covering that time period and extending quite a bit further out into the future, and that these aggregate forecasts have been approved and authorized by top management.

Well, we need to verify that the sum of the detailed forecasts matches the aggregate. It may not, because:

• The detailed forecasts in this example are generated initially by a statistical forecasting system.

• The aggregate forecasts are created using a different set of logic and are closely reviewed by a number of knowledgeable individuals before they're accepted.

There's no guarantee they'll match — even if they matched a month ago. Therefore it's essential, several times per month, to total up the detailed forecasts into product group or family forecasts and compare those totals to the aggregate forecasts. If they differ by more than a reasonable tolerance, it's necessary to bring them in line, almost always by modifying one or more detail forecasts. For more on this topic, see Chapter 3 of our book on sales forecasting[4].

Coming up in Chapter 5 — promising customer orders.

---

[4] Thomas F. Wallace and Robert A. Stahl, *Sales Forecasting: A New Approach*, 2002. Cincinnati, Ohio: T. F. Wallace & Company

Chapter 5

THE DEMAND SIDE: PART 2 —
MANAGING CUSTOMER ORDERS

Let's continue looking upward in the supply chain — toward the customers.

One of the most important things for a company to do well is promising customer orders. The ability to promise orders to customers *validly* — with dates and quantities that can and will be met — can be a significant competitive weapon. In our careers, we've seen more than a few struggling companies that had:

- great products,

- first-rate quality,

- competitive prices.

Why were they struggling? Because they couldn't ship on time. Most of their shipments went out late, or incomplete, or both. As a result, they made their customers unhappy and opened themselves up to competitive pressure. A major reason for this is that they lacked the ability to promise orders realistically.

In two of these cases, one of our colleagues was familiar with the companies. When he saw that they

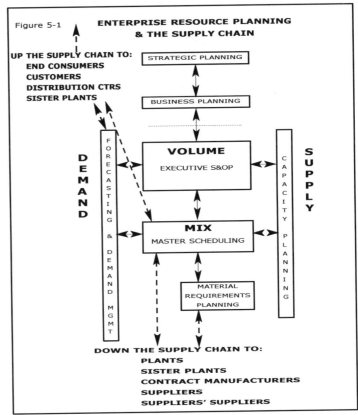

were going to solve the nagging problem of late shipments, he bought stock in both of them. Several years later, he sold Company C's stock for twelve times what he paid — a "twelve-bagger" in Wall Street jargon. He sold Company T's stock a few years after that for *sixty* times his purchase price. While both of these companies — a twelve-bagger and a sixty-bagger — did a lot of things right, superior on-time shipping performance was probably the most important factor in the stock appreciation. Bottom line: superior customer service hits the bottom line, and can heavily impact the stock price.

Available-to-Promise

In this task of promising customer orders, the Master Schedule has a major role to play. Before we get into the details, let's look at our next principle of Master Scheduling:

> **Principle #10: The Master Schedule is the basis for customer order promising, via its Available-to-Promise feature.**

Let's see how it does this by taking another look at Product #11223, which we saw in the last chapter.

In Figure 5-2, we've added two rows labeled Available-to-Promise (ATP). This is the source of customer order promising. Looking across the top ATP row, the first number we see is 29. Two questions come to mind:

- What does it mean?

- How did it get there?

Figure 5-2

MASTER SCHEDULE DISPLAY — AVAILABLE-TO-PROMISE #1

Product #11223

Week	PAST DUE	1	2	3	4	5	6	7	8
Sales Forecast		3	10	10	10	10	10	10	10
Customer Orders		7							
Total Demand		10	10	10	10	10	10	10	10
Projected Available Balance **(OHB = 36)**		26	16	6	21	11	1	16	6
Available-to-Promise									
Period		29			25			25	
Cumulative		29			54			79	
Master Production Schedule (MPS)					25F			25F	

It means that right now we can accept customer orders for up to 29 units and ship them any time the customer wants. The 29 is the result of getting the inventory number (OHB = 36) and subtracting from it the customer orders already booked but not shipped (7)[1].

You've no doubt noticed that we're showing two Available-to-Promise rows: one for the period and one on a cumulative basis. Do you need two rows on your Master Schedule display? Probably not. Which one should we use? Take your pick: period, cumulative, or both. Some people maintain that the period display is superior because it's a bit clearer, and others are concerned that the cumulative display could lead to promising the same product twice. For our purposes, we'll use the period display because it is a bit easier to follow.

We need to see some more examples of Available-to-Promise. Look back to Figure 5-2 and let's presume our customer says: "I want 18 of Product #11223 in Week 3. Can you let me have them?" What should we tell that person? Some of you might be thinking that, because the Projected Available Balance at the end of Week 3 is only 6, we can't promise 18 in Week 3[2].

However, in this case, we can handle that order for 18 in Week 3 because the Available-to-Promise shows it's okay. We have 29 available in Week 1 to cover all customer orders until Week 4, when there's more production scheduled — and hence more availability.

The Projected Available Balance, on the other hand, has been reduced by the *forecast*. Forecasts are not booked orders; they're orders we haven't gotten yet, but hope to get in the future. The forecasts should affect the Projected Available Balance but not Available-to-Promise.

Here's the distinction between the Projected Available Balance and Available-to-Promise:

- The Projected Available Balance is the critique of the demand/supply relationship. It enables us to keep the Master Production Schedules timed properly. To do this, it's necessary to factor in the forecasts as well as the sold orders.

---

[1] If they had been shipped, they would have been subtracted from the On-Hand Balance and also taken out of the Customer Order row. They would have become history.

[2] This stands in sharp contrast to the "always say yes" method. Some companies always say yes to what the customer wants, and thus accept the order not knowing whether they can ship it on time and complete. Often they can't, and they frequently disappoint the customer. On the other hand, the really excellent companies *almost always* say yes to the customer request, but *only after checking* to ensure they have product, or material and capacity, to meet that order. And then they keep their promise.

- Available-to-Promise is the source for customer order promising. It disregards the forecast. It relates booked customer orders to current supply (the on-hand inventory) and *future* supply as expressed by the Master Production Schedule.

Now let's look at Product #11223 *after* we book the customer's order for 18 in Week 3, shown in Figure 5-3. The Available-to-Promise in Week 1 has been reduced by the 18 piece order we just booked, and it's telling us that we still have 11 to promise until the Master Production Schedule in Week 4 is completed. Then we'll have more.

Figure 5-3

MASTER SCHEDULE DISPLAY — AVAILABLE-TO-PROMISE #2

Product #11223

Week	PAST DUE	1	2	3	4	5	6	7	8
Sales Forecast		3	2	0	10	10	10	10	10
Customer Orders		7		18					
Total Demand		10	2	18	10	10	10	10	10
Projected Available Balance (OHB = 36)		26	24	6	21	11	1	16	6
Available-to-Promise		11			25			25	
Master Production Schedule (MPS)					25F			25F	

In this example, the Available-to-Promise number was based on the On-Hand Balance; in other words, ATP is the uncommitted portion of the inventory. So you're thinking, "What's the big deal? We've been doing that for years." Stay tuned.

Looking to the right in the top Available-to-Promise row, we can see two additional quantities: 25 in Week 4 and 25 in Week 7. These are derived from the MPSs in the same weeks. They represent *future* inventory. Thanks to the time-phasing capabilities of the Master Schedule, in addition to the current availability, the future availability of product can be readily determined.

Most companies need this information to promise customer orders well; it's not enough to look only at available inventory in the warehouse. They need to know what's coming. This is particularly true for make-to-order products. We're looking at a make-to-stock product here, but Available-to-Promise works just as well for make-to-order, where the main difference is that *there is no finished goods inventory*. All availability is in the future.

Now, still looking at Figure 5-3, let's see if we can legitimately promise the next order, where a customer is asking for 28 units in Week 4. Can we say yes? Yes, we can. We have an Available-to-Promise of 25 in Week 4. That covers all but 3 of the customer order. Well, what about the remaining 3 units? Should those come out of the 25 available in Week 7? No, that's too late; the customer wants her order in Week 4 and she wants it complete. The other 3 need to come out of the 11 available in Week 1.

In Figure 5-4, we can see how the Master Schedule would look after we book this order.

Figure 5-4

MASTER SCHEDULE DISPLAY — AVAILABLE-TO-PROMISE #3

Product #11223

Week	PAST DUE	1	2	3	4	5	6	7	8
Sales Forecast		0	0	0	0	0	7	10	10
Customer Orders	7			18	**28**				
Total Demand	**7**	**0**	18	28	**0**	7	10	10	
Projected Available Balance (OHB = 36)		29	29	11	8	8	1	16	6
Available-to-Promise	**8**				0			25	
Master Production Schedule (MPS)					25F			25F	

A question arises: Shouldn't the logic of Available-to-Promise have used all of the availability in Week 1 — all 11 — before taking any of the 25 in Week 4? Not really. The reason is that it tries to save early availability until it's needed. In this case, the Week 4 availability of 25 should be used to satisfy as much of the Week 4 demand as possible — and only then go after the availability in Week 1. That way we protect our close-in availability in case another customer asks us to respond quickly.

Decision Making

For our next example, let's suppose a good customer calls up and says they need a dozen of Product #11223 in Week 6. Can we do it? There are two answers to this question: no and maybe. The "no" answer comes from what our Available-to-Promise is saying: Out through Week 6, all we have available is the 8 in Week 1. "No" is the mechanical response to the question.

The "maybe" answer involves human judgment and ingenuity. It calls up another question: What might be done in order to get this good customer the amount of our product that s/he's asking for at the time s/he wants it? Here are some possibilities:

- Move the MPS in Week 7 into Week 6.

- Split the MPS in Week 7 and move a small part of it (4 or more) into Week 6.

- Add a new MPS for four in Week 6.

- Increase the MPS in Week 4 by four.

- Contact one or more of the customers who have orders for this product, for example the one who's ordered 28 in Week 4. See if they could live with four less for a few weeks.

- Investigate substituting another product for Product #11223, perhaps a more expensive one with the same functionality but more features. Consider offering that one to the customer at the same price as #11223.

Who should do this research and make the decision? Certainly not the computer. A human being, and probably more than one. Probably the Master Scheduler would be most involved with the first three possibilities and someone from Sales & Marketing would work on the last two options.

Please note: *The computer can say "yes" but it can't say "no."* When the Available-to-Promise won't cover the incoming demand, it's the computer's job to call out the problem to the human beings whose job it is to handle these cases. It's their job to learn the specifics of the situation, communicate with the involved parties, and make a decision.

In our book on Sales Forecasting, your friendly authors stated that "Available-to-Promise *does not make decisions to ship or not to ship. It does not make decisions on which customer gets product in limited supply.* Its job is to fill the demand where supply is available — now or in the future — and when that's not possible, to kick it out to *human beings for evaluation and decision making.* If you're starting to think that this is a high-communication process, you're absolutely right. Companies who do this well communicate intensively among the Master Scheduler(s), Sales, Production, Purchasing, and — where appropriate — top management."

A few paragraphs ago, we used the phrase "someone from Sales & Marketing." Who might that someone be? Many companies have established a position called "Demand Manager," who is frequently given responsibility for working closely with the Master Scheduler on demand/supply problems. A sample job description for the Demand Manager is contained in Appendix C.

Now let's pretend that the pending customer order for 12 in Week 6 was booked without changing anything else. In other words, someone decided to enter the order, thereby violating the Available-to-Promise (ATP) quantities. Figure 5-5 shows how it would look.

Figure 5-5

MASTER SCHEDULE DISPLAY — NEGATIVE ATP

Product #11223 Lead Time = 1 week Order Quantity = 25
Planning Time Fence @ Week 7

Week	PAST DUE	1	2	3	4	5	6	7	PTF 8
Sales Forecast							**0**	**8**	10
Customer Orders		7		18	28		**12**		
Total Demand		7		18	28		**12**	**8**	10
Projected Available Balance (OHB = 36)		29	29	11	8	8	**-4**	**13**	**3**
Available-to-Promise		8			0		**-4**	25	
Master Production Schedule (MPS)					25F			25F	

Action Message: ATP negative in Week 6
Reschedule MPS Week 7 to Week 6

This is how the Master Scheduling software calls attention to the problem that's been created. In effect, it's saying, "If things go the way you have planned them, you will run out of product in Week 6. You will not have enough to keep your promises to your customers."

It's then up to the human beings to solve the problem — and perhaps they're well on their way to doing that. Perhaps they've already identified how they're going to handle this — maybe by moving in some or all of the Master Production Schedule of 25 in Week 7 — and are merely waiting for the details to emerge before they enter the new plan. On the other hand, perhaps the latest customer order was entered inadvertently and they have some homework to do to figure out the recovery.

That raises another issue that must be addressed, after the smoke clears: How did the bad promise get made in the first place? Finding the root cause and taking corrective action may very well prevent other bad promises from being made again in the future.

Multiple Products per Order

Many companies receive orders containing more than one product — or "order line" as they're sometimes called. In these cases, effective order promising involves looking at all the individual lines on the order to determine when the *order* can be shipped complete, meaning all items on the order shipped for the full amounts specified on the order.

Let's look at an incoming order calling for three items: 10 each of Products A, B, and C with the requested delivery on Monday, June 5. Product A is okay and so is Product B. Product C will not be available until Thursday, June 8[4]. We investigate and determine it's not possible to move up Product C; there's a critical component that won't be available.

We check with the customer, explain the situation to them, and they agree to take their order on Thursday rather than Monday. We book it for then, taking care that this order for Product A and B is set for Thursday not Monday. Why? Because we don't need to ship the order until Thursday. By showing the orders then, we may free up availability earlier in the week for orders yet to arrive.

Some of you may be thinking, "Why not reserve the inventory of Products A and B right now to make sure that when Product C shows up, you'll be able to ship complete?" Well, if you do that, you'll be tying up inventory — unnecessarily, if you believe the Master Schedule. If you don't trust the Master Schedule to represent future reality, then you have a much larger problem. Making the Master Schedule believable, and having people trust what it tells them, is central to running this part of the business well.

---

[4] As we saw, many companies will maintain their Master Schedule in *daily* time periods, especially during the first week or two.

Mini Case: A Producer of Telecommunications Equipment. Company M had an excellent Master Scheduling process and they did a fine job with customer order promising. Most of their orders contained more than one product though, which caused them a bit of a problem because of differences in customer preferences.

Some customers didn't want partial shipments; they wanted their orders to be shipped complete. Other customers wanted as much of their order as soon as possible, and were willing to live with backorders. How did they deal with this dilemma?

Well, Company M customized their order entry and Master Scheduling software to:

- contain a code for each customer that specified whether the customer wanted complete shipments or was okay with partials,

- make the Available-to-Promise logic verify that code prior to checking availability,

- have the ATP logic promise orders on that basis. If a given customer was okay with partials, it promised the individual products irrespective of a complete order. Conversely, if the customer wanted complete orders, it promised those items accordingly.

The name of the game is to keep the customers happy. Company M's excellent approach to customer order promising is one way to do just that.

Multiple Order Entry Points

Available-to-Promise is an effective, eminently logical way to promise customer orders. However, its widespread adoption has come later than it should have. Why is that?

One reason is that it's taken quite some time for many companies to get their Master Scheduling practices on track and effective. Promises made from a bad Master Schedule will almost certainly be bad promises.

Another problem has been software. If the order entry software is on a given software platform and the Master Scheduling is on another, it's difficult to get them to talk to each other. Available-to-Promise requires, in almost all companies, that they do talk to each other.

A third problem arises when a company has multiple locations where customer orders are entered. Companies with more than one order entry point can run the risk of promising the same availability twice. For example, the order entry person in Des Moines might promise an order at 10:00 a.m., and her counterpart in Dallas might be looking at the same item at 10:30. If the data has not been updated in the interim, the guy in Dallas could inadvertently make an invalid promise. Therefore, the ATP function in environments like this needs to operate in *real time*. The entire system must instantly update itself at time of entry.

Please allow us to digress for just a moment. The track record of Enterprise Resource Planning software — more validly called Enterprise-wide Systems — has been, at best, mixed. Thousands of companies have spent billions of dollars to install this software with not much to show in the way of results (except for a relatively few unique cases). Here's a piece of good news to offset some of the bad: Enterprise-wide Systems are one of the best things that ever happened to Available-to-Promise. They provide capabilities that in the past were tough to come by: multiple users sharing files and updating them on-line in real time.

So here's an opportunity to recoup some of that enormous investment that your company may have made in its enterprise-wide software. Get your Master Schedule under control and valid, and then use Available-to-Promise to do a first-rate job of promising orders to your customers. Few things in a manufacturing enterprise are more important.

Capable-to-Promise

In recent years, we've seen the advent of an advanced form of Available-to-Promise. It's called Capable-to-Promise, and here's how the two differ:

- Available-to-Promise tells us when current or *future* inventory of finished product will be available to ship to customers. It does this by relating customer orders already booked to inventory on hand and Master Production Schedules.

- Capable-to-Promise, contained in some software products, kicks in when Available-to-Promise isn't adequate to cover the requested customer demand. It asks:

1. Could we set up a new Master Production Schedule to meet this demand? Let's call this one MPS #2. Do we have capacity and material available to produce MPS #2?

2. If not, could we take some capacity and material allocated to an existing Master Production Schedule for another product (MPS #1) which is perhaps not needed as urgently? Perhaps all or a portion of MPS #1 is for stock replenishment and not for covering any sold customer orders. Or perhaps a portion of MPS #1 is lot sized; for example when we run this product, we try to run four week's supply. Perhaps we could "borrow" material and capacity from MPS #1 and thus make running MPS #2 doable.

These steps are valid and logical. You readers who've done Master Scheduling are probably nodding your heads — you've done these things manually. It's part of the job. The Capable-to-Promise software feature partially automates what can otherwise be a complex and time consuming step. It can make it easier to say "yes we can" to a customer — and mean it.

Abnormal Demand Control

It's Tuesday morning in the Customer Service Department and things are in fine shape. Business is strong; the customers are happy; the stock price is up; and our favorite baseball team just won two out of three against the Yankees.

The phone rings and it's a customer: the Adams Company. They're interested in buying 75 of our Product #99887, and they'd like them in Week 6. Can we deliver? We check the Available-to-Promise (see Figure 5-6).

Well, according to the ATP, we can say yes. We have 53 and 25 available through Week 5, so we can meet their request of 75 in Week 6. But do we necessarily want to do that? Perhaps there are a few questions that need to be answered first before we make a commitment. Who are these Adams people anyway? Are they an existing customer, one who's been with us for a while? Or is this the first time we've ever heard from them? Maybe they're coming to us only because their supplier's plant had a fire and is out of commission for a while.

In this latter case, the Adams order is quite possibly a "one-time shot." On the one hand, once their supplier's plant is back on line, we may never see them again. On the other hand, this may be an opportunity to help the Adams Company out of a jam, to make a friend, and perhaps to lay the groundwork for an ongoing relationship.

Figure 5-6

MASTER SCHEDULE DISPLAY — ABNORMAL DEMAND

Product #99887

Week	1	2	3	4	5	6	7	8
Sales Forecast	20	13		5		20	20	20
Customer Orders			27		35			
Total Demand	20	13	27	5	35	20	20	20
Projected Available Balance 80	60	47	20	15	40	20	0	40
Available-to-Promise (ATP)	53				25			60
Master Production Schedule (MPS)					60			60

So, there's good news and bad news about abnormal demand. The good news is that it's a chance for increased sales and it's an opportunity to acquire a new and continuing customer. The downside of abnormal demand is that, unless managed properly, it can cause problems. We may miss shipments to existing customers because we're diverting resources to the abnormal order. Also, the abnormal order itself may not be shipped on time or complete, due to pressure from existing customers for their orders.

Please note the words "managed properly." That's the key to this abnormal demand business: managing it effectively. Let's raise some questions:

- *What is abnormal demand?* Typically it's demand that's not in the forecast. It also tends to be random, non-recurring, and highly variable. The word "lumpy" is often used to describe it.

- *How to detect it?* Most often, abnormal demand orders show up on a nontypical basis because they come from customers with whom the company has not been doing business. More often than not, they come in by means other than the company's normal order entry processes.

In companies where abnormal demand is likely to enter via the normal order entry channels, it's a good idea to have some kind of filter built into the order entry system prior to Available-to-Promise time. One simple approach is to use a percentage of one month's forecast. In other words, if the forecast is 150 and the filter is set at 50 percent — half of one month's volume, i.e. 75 — then an incoming order for 100 would be kicked out to a human being for a decision.

A more rigorous method for setting these filters is to base them statistically on the variability of demand against the forecast. Companies use a multiple of the Mean Absolute Deviation (MAD) to do this. A discussion of the MAD is contained in Appendix E, which deals with Safety Stock and Safety Time.

- *Who decides what to do?* Here again, we place the decision-making responsibility with Sales. These folks are by far the best equipped to make a decision that might help the company acquire a new customer but could negatively impact current customers. These decisions should not be left up to the folks in Operations because they're just not as close to the customers.

  Operations should, however, have an advisory role. Sales needs to hear from Operations about its ability to meet the abnormal demand while protecting current customer commitments and other demands. Once again, interdepartmental communication is critical.

There's another set of questions to be asked. These are ones the decision-makers need to answer while making their decision:

- *Is this order part of the forecast?* Most times, when dealing with abnormal demand, the answer will be no. This means that it offers the opportunity for incremental business but may cause capacity and material problems in Operations. If the abnormal demand is actually in the forecast but slated for different time periods, then dealing with it typically presents less of a resource challenge; material and capacity are or will be available, and the main issue might be one of timing. In our example above, the Adams order was not part of the forecast[3].

- *What is the impact on other customers?* This is the information owed by Operations. They might say that in order to ship Adams complete, we'd have to short the Smith order by 30 percent and we'll be a week late shipping the order for Ajax. However, if Adams can get by with less, we should be able to protect both the Smith and Ajax orders.

---

[3] If an order not in the forecast is accepted, it should not consume the forecast. On the other hand, if the order is in the forecast but in different time periods, then that forecast should be consumed.

- *What does the customer really need?* Does Adams really need all 75 in Week 6? Or perhaps do they need 10 per week beginning in Week 6 for eight weeks? If so, this is an entirely different situation and one that should be much easier to deal with. Well, if Adams doesn't need all 75 in Week 6, why would they order that way? We don't know, but it happens frequently. Maybe they were trying to be helpful by "bothering" us with only one order versus eight. Maybe they're concerned about having to process eight shipments versus one, and the related freight costs. Maybe we give a price break when a customer orders 75 and they're responding to that.

Finding out *what the customer really needs* is a key part of managing abnormal demand.

One detail to keep in mind: These orders need to be uniquely coded to identify them as abnormal, both while they're active — so that they don't automatically consume the forecast — and later when they're sent to the demand history file.

Regarding the latter point on demand history: The statistical forecasting system needs to know that it should ignore abnormal demand orders as it makes forecasts based on past demand patterns. If not, it will roll the demand into the forecast, when in fact abnormal demand for specific items is not repetitive. However, and this important, if the abnormal demand came from a company who subsequently becomes an ongoing customer, then the sales history should probably be adjusted to include that demand.

To resolve this issue and to make the right call might require a fair amount of time by the person in Sales & Marketing charged with the decision-making responsibility. Certainly it will necessitate talking with Operations, making phone calls to the Adams company, and possibly making phone calls or sending e-mails to current customers such as Smith and Ajax. One of the items often seen in Demand Managers' job descriptions is to help resolve abnormal demand issues.

A final point, for those of you who sometimes complain bitterly about how inaccurate the forecasts are: In many cases, there was nothing wrong with the forecast; it's just that a big lump of abnormal demand arrived and it *was not managed properly*. So, instead of spending lots of time, effort, and money on getting the forecasts "accurate," the company might be far better off by setting up good processes for handling abnormal demand — and then managing the business accordingly.

Chapter 6

THE SUPPLY SIDE: PART 1 —
CAPACITY AND MATERIAL PLANNING

Looking downward in the supply chain, we can see internal elements (the plants) and external ones (the suppliers). Let's turn first to the plants.

Rough-Cut Capacity Planning

Remember the saying back in Chapter 1: "You can't put ten pounds of potatoes in a five-pound bag." And it's correct — no matter how much we'd like to squeeze another five pounds into the bag, no matter how hard we try, no matter how much trouble we'll be in if we don't do it — at the end of the day, ten pounds won't fit.

It stands to reason that we'd better have a pretty good handle on two things:

1. How big is our bag (capacity)?

2. How much are we trying to put into the bag (the demand for capacity)?

Then we can compare one to the other and see if we're okay or not. The jargon of the trade identifies this as Capacity Planning. Before we launch into the details, let's take a look at the next Master Scheduling principle:

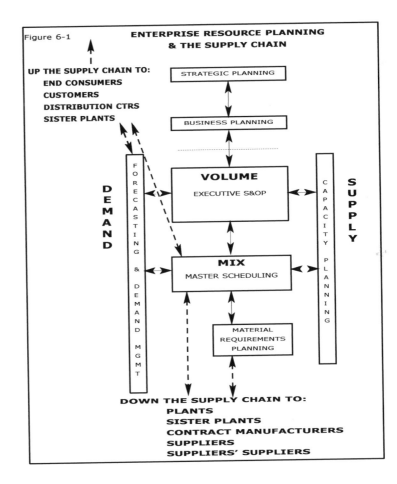

Figure 6-1

Principle # 11: Effective Capacity Planning processes are necessary to ensure that supply is in balance with demand.

A Simple Example — One Product, One Resource

In some environments, Capacity Planning is easy to do. Let's take the case of a production resource; it could be a work center, or an entire department, or a sub-department. Let's use Manufacturing Cell A1, making only one model of Widget, #44556. In fact, Manufacturing Cell A1 is the only production resource in the company, and Widget #44556 is its only product.

In this case, the capacity planning task is easy: We compare the number of Model #44556 widgets in the Master Schedule to the number of widgets that Cell A1 is capable of making. We're either okay or we're not. If we're okay, fine. If we need more widgets than the cell can produce, we must change something. We can either:

- increase the size of the bag, i.e., the capacity of the cell, or

- decrease what we're trying to stuff into the bag, i.e., reduce the demand for capacity.

Doing the latter means reducing the Master Schedule, which can mean not supporting actual demand (customer orders) or future demand (the forecast). In most cases, this course is considered a last resort, and is taken only after all other options have been exhausted.

This Capacity Planning process is a classic case of balancing demand and supply. We must get and keep the supply of capacity in balance with the demand for it.

DEMAND
FOR
CAPACITY
(from Master Schedule)

SUPPLY
OF
CAPACITY
(demonstrated output
capability)

80 widgets in Week 2

80 widgets/week

Three Products, One Resource

Okay, so not many companies have the kind of arrangement we just saw, with only one product and one work center. Almost every manufacturing enterprise has a more complex arrangement than this, and that brings up the need for a more robust Capacity Planning process.

Let's complicate our example just a bit. Let's say that Cell B4 makes not one but three different models of widgets, and normally produces about 100 of them per week. These three widgets differ from one another in their complexity and hence the amount of time required to produce them:

Widget	Production Time Required
5555A	0.5 hours
5555B	1.0 "
5555C	3.0 "

In this case, to do the Capacity Planning evaluation in units (number of widgets) probably won't work because of the very different work content of the widgets. To say that we have a workload of 100 widgets doesn't tell us much, and could get us into trouble if we assume that Cell B4 can make 100 widgets *of any specific mix*. We would need to know how many of these are "half-hour" widgets and how many take one hour and three hours.

Widget	Production Time Required per Unit	MPSs in Week 3	Production Time Required in Week 3
5555A	0.5 hours	40 units	20 hours
5555B	1.0 "	20 "	20 "
5555C	3.0 "	40 "	120 "
		100 "	160 "

Then we'd need to compare the total number of hours to the amount of hours the cell or work center is capable of producing. That comparison would tell us whether we were okay or we had a problem.

Note: This degree of detail is, in most cases, necessary only out to the Planning Time Fence. But, some of you might be wondering, what if we want to see the expected workload out beyond that Fence? Where does that come from?

The quick answer is that it's derived from the aggregate Production Plan (in most cases an output from Executive S&OP). We'll talk more about this important topic later in this chapter.

DEMAND
FOR
CAPACITY
(from Master Schedule)

SUPPLY
OF
CAPACITY
(demonstrated output
capability)

130 hours/week

160 hours in Week 3

Do we have a problem here? Maybe. Demand is certainly exceeding supply. Probably the first question to ask is how readily can we increase the supply of capacity to 160 hours in Week 3? It might be something as simple as overtime: perhaps ten-hour shifts, and/or work the weekend. Or maybe we can offload some of this work to alternate work centers.

But what if those tactics won't work? Let's say that Cell B4 is maxed out; it's already running 24/7. Further, it may be that B4 is the only production resource anywhere, inside or outside of our plant, that can make these products. Then the picture shown above is a major problem. We cannot increase the supply of capacity and thus we must reduce the demand. This means going into the Master Schedule and reducing run quantities and/or changing the timing of one or more orders to another week where open capacity exists.

Please note: Our example showed a schedule that called for 100 units from a cell that typically could produce 100 units in a week. On the surface, that sounds as if everything's okay. Only when we "translated" the units into hours did the overload problem become visible. For most work centers in most companies, hours are the preferred unit of measure.

Four Products, Three Resources

The Northern Bleen Swivel Company (NoBS) has a plant in Wisconsin that makes the upper end of their product line, which includes six specific products. There are three primary resources in the plant: Assembly, Fabrication 1, and Fabrication 2.

The folks at Northern have constructed what's called a "Bill of Resources," (also called a "Load Profile") shown in Figure 6-2. This can be done in a matrix format, to show the relationship between the products and the resources in terms of resource consumption. Let's take a look.

Figure 6-2

BILL OF RESOURCES
HOURS REQUIRED PER 1,000 UNITS

Product #	Assembly	Fab 1	Fab 2
1234	2.1	2.8	1.1
3456	6.5	0.2	1.5
5678	3.7	8.5	3.5
7890	0.9	2.0	5.2

In other words, it takes 2.1 hours in Assembly to make 1,000 units of Product #1234, 2.8 hours in Fab 1, and so forth. These numbers were derived from standards, and are periodically reviewed for validity, perhaps several times per year. Sometimes things change, and one can't assume that these averages will stay the same forever.

To determine the workload in any given week, simply multiply the bill of resources data by the amount of each product master scheduled. Let's say that, in Week 2, we have Master Production Schedules as follows:

Product 1234 – 1,000 units
"   3456 – 2,000   "
"   5678 – 3,000   "
"   7890 – 4,000   "

Laying those MPS quantities for Week 2 into the bill of resources results in the picture shown in Figure 6-3. This is the *demand* for capacity; what's needed now is the supply. Well, these three resources are currently operating for one eight-hour shift per day, five days per week. That equals 40 hours, but — and this is a big "but" — these are not the same kind of hours as those in Figure 6-2. The 40 hours are *clock* hours, while our calculated workload above is in *standard* hours. Comparing these is just not valid; it's the proverbial apples to oranges comparison.

What we need to know is the capacity of these resources in *standard* hours. This raises the question of how efficient these resources are. If a given resource were 100 percent efficient, then in 80 clock hours it would produce 80 *standard hours* of work (number of good units produced times the standard hours per unit)[1].

Figure 6-3

STANDARD HOURS REQUIRED
IN WEEK 2

Product MPS Qty	Assembly	Fab 1	Fab 2
1234 – 1,000	2.1	2.8	1.1
3456 – 2,000	13.0	0.4	3.0
5678 – 3,000	11.1	25.5	10.5
7890 – 4,000	3.6	8.0	20.8
TOTALS	29.8	36.7	35.4

In our example, Assembly is 90 percent efficient, Fab 1 is 60 percent efficient, and Fab 2 is 96 percent efficient. Since these resources are operating 40 clock hours per week, we can predict their average output over time — called demonstrated capacity — to be:

Assembly = 36 standard hours (40 times 90%)
Fab 1   = 24   ”   ”   (40 times 60%)
Fab 2   = 38.4 ”   ”   (40 times 96%)

Now let's compare the standard hours required (demand for capacity) to the demonstrated capacity (supply) for these resources. See Figure 6-4.

Hmmm, maybe things here aren't as trouble-free as they appeared when we looked only at clock hours. We can see that Fab 1 has a demand/supply problem, and that some action will have to be taken or this schedule will not be produced. Right now, the situation at Fab 1 is pretty much ten pounds in a five-pound bag.

---

[1] Different companies have various terms and calculations for what we've called efficiency factors. This can be a complex topic, with some companies employing utilization and other factors beyond just the simple efficiency factors we've talked about here. The important point is that the clock hours should be factored to properly represent reality.

Figure 6-4

ROUGH-CUT CAPACITY PLAN
WEEK 2 — IN STANDARD HOURS

Product MPS Qty	Assembly	Fab 1	Fab 2
1234 – 1,000	2.1	2.8	1.1
3456 – 2,000	13.0	0.4	3.0
5678 – 3,000	11.1	25.5	10.5
7890 – 4,000	3.6	8.0	20.8
TOTALS	29.8	36.7	35.4
DEMONSTRATED CAPACITY	36.0	24.0	38.4

But hold on a minute, a conscientious reader (CR) might be thinking: *The problem at Fab 1 is that their efficiency is terrible; they're running at only 60 percent.*

Our response: *And . . . ?*

CR: *But if they just got their act together and started to run better, there wouldn't be a problem.*

Our response: *When will that happen?*

CR: *Well, something oughta be done. They should at least get started on the problem.*

We agree, but that's a somewhat different issue. There are two things on the table here: 1) creating valid schedules, and 2) fixing the efficiency problem at Fab 1. Regarding the schedule for Week 2, all we can count on now is about 24 standard hours of output. That's their *demonstrated* capacity; it's what Fab 1 has proven it can do. For the schedule to be valid, it had better recognize that reality. (Reality is frequently a pain in the butt, but it's usually not a good idea to ignore it.)

When the folks in Fab 1 improve their processes, when they have proven that they can sustain higher outputs with no increase in clock hours, when they have demonstrated their ability to produce at a higher efficiency rate over some period of time, then it'll be time to increase Fab 1's demonstrated capacity number. In the meantime, wishful thinking makes for two problems — bad efficiency compounded by bad scheduling.

Displays

What we're seeing in Figure 6-4 is one way to display Capacity Planning information. Note the approach: We're looking at a number of resources (Assembly, Fab 1, Fab 2) for only one time period (Week 2).

Another way to view it is to focus on only one resource over a number of time periods, as shown in Figure 6-5.

Figure 6-5

FAB 1 — ROUGH-CUT CAPACITY PLAN

	Week 1	Week 2	Week 3	Week 4	Week 5	Week 6
Workload	33.9	36.7	35.5	40.9	29.1	32.1
Demo. Cap.	24.0	24.0	24.0	24.0	24.0	24.0
Difference	-9.9	-12.7	-11.5	-16.9	-5.1	-8.1
Cumulative	-9.9	-22.6	-34.1	-51.0	-56.1	-64.2

It goes without saying that Fab 1 is in terrible shape for the foreseeable future. What else is in terrible shape is the Master Schedule that's calling for far more than what Fab 1 can produce. Actually it's not really a Master Schedule; it's a wish list.

One advantage of this display is that it shows what's likely to happen in a given resource over time. That can help in problem identification and resolution. In the example in Figure 6-5, these numbers should point the Master Scheduler toward looking for additional resources (alternate work centers, outside subcontractors, and so forth) — and quickly.

Another way to display this information is in a graphical format, as opposed to the tabular view we've been using. In Figure 6-6, we can see the same information as in Figure 6-5 displayed graphically.

Please note that the displays in Figures 6-4, 6-5, and 6-6 do not show which MPSs are making up the workload. There will be times, however, when the Master Scheduler or others (frequently plant people) will absolutely have to see that level of detail for problem diagnosis and solution. A well-constructed set of Master Scheduling software will make it very easy to call up the detail, and to view it along with the summary information. Most people prefer to view summary capacity information in this graphical format, and to see the details on a tabular basis.

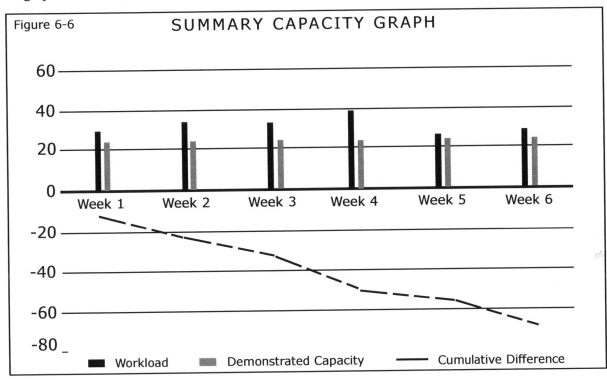

Figure 6-6 SUMMARY CAPACITY GRAPH

Workload ▪ Demonstrated Capacity ▪ Cumulative Difference —

Relieving Overloads

What courses of action exist to solve overload problems? Actually, there are quite a few.

- Overtime.
- Use an alternate resource (work center, line, cell, plant).
- Subcontract.
- Add people.
- Add equipment.
- Substitute existing product (for what's in the current, overloaded schedule).
- Cut order quantities.
- Run some product earlier.
- Run some product later, but still meet the schedule by compressing selected lead times.

And lastly, when all else fails, reschedule out some of the customer orders. In most of the suggested alternatives, good Capacity Planning information can be essential for making the right decisions.

Other Types of Capacity Planning

We need to look briefly at several other types of capacity planning, primarily to help you keep all this stuff sorted out. You may hear these terms from time to time.

Resource Requirements Planning

This is a term used by APICS which means almost the same thing as Rough-Cut Capacity Planning. The main difference, as we understand it, is that Rough-Cut Capacity Planning is done in conjunction with the Master Production Schedule while Resource Requirements Planning is tied to the Production Plan in Executive S&OP.

We don't believe this distinction is enough to warrant a different term. The mechanics of these techniques are identical. The use of the tools is virtually the same. Why have two terms to define the same thing? We believe that there are enough (too many?) terms in this field already. Let's keep it simple and make it easier for the people coming into the field to learn the important things.

Figure 6-7 shows the differences in the use of Rough-Cut Capacity Planning when done in conjunction with the Production Plan and with the Master Schedule.

Figure 6-7

CHARACTERISTICS OF ROUGH-CUT CAPACITY PLANNING (RCCP)

Characteristic	Using Production Plan	Using Master Schedule
Driven By	Families	End Items/Modules
Horizon	15–36 Months	4–16 Weeks
Time Periods	Primarily Months	Primarily Days or Weeks
Detail	Only Key Resources	Many Resources

Capacity Requirements Planning (CRP)

This tool is used mainly in complex, job shop manufacturing environments typically involving many work centers, deep bills of material, complex routings, long lead times, and so on. It differs from Rough-Cut Capacity Planning in that its calculations are much more detailed. It is similar to Rough-Cut in that the use of the two tools is much the same: The users can see potential bottlenecks ahead of time and thus can take corrective action to eliminate them or to schedule around them.

The use of CRP has declined. More and more companies have simplified their manufacturing environments, thanks to approaches such as Just-in-Time and Lean Manufacturing, and simpler environments don't need detailed Capacity Requirements Planning. That doesn't mean that they don't need to validate their Master Schedule with regard to capacity. Rather, the tools they use to do that are much simpler.

Infinite Loading

This is merely another term — and an old one — for Capacity Requirements Planning. What it meant was that the computer calculated the future workload *independently* of capacity and then displayed the results to the human beings involved so that they could solve the bottlenecks, overloads, underloads, and so on.

The anti-MRP crowd jumped on this, claiming that "MRP assumes infinite capacity, and therefore it's no good." Nonsense. MRP didn't assume infinite anything, because obviously there's no such thing as an infinite supply of capacity. CRP (infinite loading, if you prefer) calculates the workload irrespective of capacity and displays the information to the people involved so they can make the right decisions on overloads, bottlenecks, offloading, alternate routings, and the like.

Finite Loading

This is an extension of "infinite loading." The computer first calculates the load on an infinite basis (as in CRP) and identifies the overloads and underloads. It then fills in the valleys (underloads) with the peaks (overloads).

Finite loading initially didn't work very well. The problem was that to shift the workload meant to change the due dates of the production orders involved. Doing this violated the priorities that were set by Master Scheduling and MRP. The plant had a nice level load, but it was no longer producing matched sets of parts. The supply side was optimized but the demand side took a bad hit: the inability to ship on time.

The good news is that these early attempts at finite loading led to the development of what are now called Finite Scheduling software packages. They work, and we'll talk about those in the next chapter.

Rough-Cut Material Planning

As companies make the transition to Lean Manufacturing, they make their production linear and dramatically lean out their inventories. Many find that they no longer need to use Material Requirements Planning to order materials from suppliers. Rather, they are able to use the Kanban approach (see Appendix F, Lean Manufacturing) to trigger replenishment shipments from their vendors. Some of these companies, however, continue to use MRP for longer range planning, so that they can give the suppliers information for their Capacity Planning. This approach is fine.

However, there's an even simpler way to do it: explode rough-cut material requirements off of the Master Schedule for short-to medium-term requirements — and off of the Production Plan for longer-term needs.

Figure 6-8 shows an example of a material profile. Multiplying this set of data by the Master Production Schedule enables the company to calculate future needs for materials and communicate them to their suppliers. It operates in much the same way as Rough-Cut Capacity Planning. Will these calculations be as precise as those that would come from MRP? Probably not. Does it matter? Probably not.

Figure 6-8

MATERIAL PROFILE
VENDOR M987
POUNDS REQUIRED PER 1,000 UNITS

Product #	Material A	Material B	Material C
1234		2.8	1.1
3456	6.5		1.5
5678		8.5	3.5
7890	0.9	2.0	

Rough-Cut Material Planning at the Master Schedule level is probably not a good practice for companies operating traditionally, as opposed to being in Lean mode. The reason is based on inventories of materials and components:

- In Lean, they're virtually nonexistent. Therefore they can safely be ignored, which is what Rough-Cut does.

- In traditional manufacturing, these inventories can be substantial. Ignoring them might cause bad information to be generated. MRP, using a traditional bill of material explosion, would be the better approach because it recognizes existing inventories and nets against them to calculate future material requirements.

These comments apply to Rough-Cut Material Planning off of the Master Schedule. However, this technique used with the Production Plan (out of Executive S&OP) is perfectly appropriate for both traditional companies as well as Lean ones. For the traditional company, then, their future material requirements would be calculated by MRP out through the Planning Time Fence and beyond by Rough-Cut Material Planning off of the Production Plan. See Figure 6-9.

Please note the bottom row. It says that Rough-Cut Material Planning off of the Production Plan is the approach to use for all companies when they're projecting supplier requirements beyond the Planning Time Fence.

This is an important point. As we said back in Chapter 3, it's what enables the horizon of the Master Schedule to be fairly short: a matter of several weeks or months, as opposed to an entire year or more.

Figure 6-9

COMPARISON OF ORDERING AND PLANNING METHODS IN TRADITIONAL AND LEAN MANUFACTURING

	TRADITIONAL	LEAN
Releasing orders to suppliers	MRP and/or Supplier Scheduling	Kanban
Planning Info for suppliers inside the Planning Time Fence	MRP and/or Supplier Scheduling	Rough-Cut Material Planning off of the Master Schedule
Planning Info for suppliers outside the Planning Time Fence	Rough-Cut Material Planning off of the Production Plan	Rough-Cut Material Planning off of the Production Plan

Chapter 7

THE SUPPLY SIDE: PART 2 — SCHEDULES FOR PLANTS AND SUPPLIERS

The Master Schedule is not normally used directly as the schedule for the plant. It's not really intended as such. On the one hand, the Master Schedule contains information that plant floor personnel usually aren't concerned with (item forecasts, inventory projections, order promising information, and so forth). On the other hand, the Master Schedule normally lacks details that the plant needs, as we'll see in just a moment.

The Finishing Schedule

It's time to take another look at the Resource Planning chart we saw earlier (see Figure 7-1). Toward the bottom of the figure, you can see a line leading downward from the Master Scheduling box to the area showing the downstream supply chain: plants and suppliers. This is where the Finishing Schedule[1] resides; for the plants and contract manufacturers, it lays out the details of which finished products are to be built and when.

Here's our next principle of Master Scheduling:

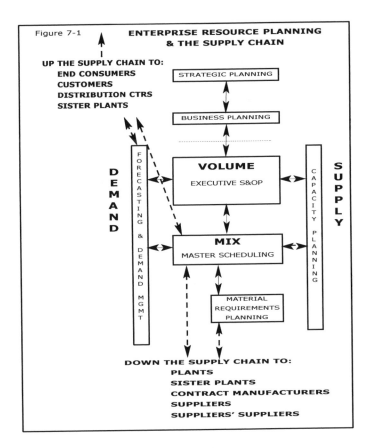

Principle #12: The Master Schedule and the Finishing Schedule are rarely the same thing. The Finishing Schedule is derived from the Master schedule and is focused on short-term supply.

---

[1] Often called the "Final Assembly Schedule." We prefer Finishing Schedule because it is broader and more inclusive. Final Assembly Schedule carries with it a connotation of products assembled out of piece parts. Many products aren't finished that way; they're mixed, blended, filled, extruded, packaged, and so on.

Here's how they differ:

- The mission of the Master Schedule is to balance demand and supply at the mix level, thus assuring material and capacity availability. The mission of the Finishing Schedule is to assign specific products and orders to specific resources and to establish the sequence and timing of those jobs.

- The Master Schedule is normally expressed in weekly time buckets, or a mix of daily and weekly increments. The Finishing Schedule is usually shown by day, by shift, and sometimes by hour. In some Lean Manufacturing environments, this schedule could be communicated in increments as small as ten minutes.

- The Master Schedule shows the picture on demand and supply. The Finishing Schedule typically focuses on supply only.

- The horizon of the Master Schedule extends to or beyond the Planning Time Fence, usually four to twelve weeks into the future. The Finishing Schedule typically goes out no more than a week or two into the future, and can be as short as a few shifts.

In his comprehensive book, *Master Scheduling*[2], John Proud states: "The finishing schedule establishes work authorization — i.e., approval to perform work on defined products, using specified capacity and materials — according to a schedule that identifies the sequence in which the work is to be performed. The finishing schedule sets priorities for finishing, assembly, filling, testing, packaging, and so forth."

John goes on to say that the Finishing Schedule can exist in a number of different formats, which of course will vary from plant to plant. These include line schedules, work center sequence lists, work orders, scheduling boards, Kanbans, and load-leveling boxes[3], among others.

In Figure 7-2 we can see a simplified sample of a Finishing Schedule, perhaps one for the filling and packaging department of a pharmaceutical plant. You can see that the focus here is on the supply side — what to make — with a very high degree of detail. Specific jobs (identified by lot numbers) are assigned to resources (lines). When to take changeovers is specified.

---

[2] John F. Proud, *Master Scheduling: A Practical Guide to Competitive Manufacturing, Second Edition,* New York: John Wiley & Sons, 1999.

[3] For a brief description of Kanban and other tools used in Lean Manufacturing , see Appendix F.

Figure 7-2

Finishing Schedule for Week Beginning 5-23

Line 1:	**1st Shift**	**2nd Shift**
Monday	Product #: 9134 Qty: 12,000 Lot #: A175	Complete Lot A175 Product #: 2468 Qty: 6,000 Lot #: S453
Tuesday	Product #: 4357 Qty: 24,000 Lot #: R292	Run R292
Wednesday	Complete R292 Product #: 2567 Qty: 16,000 Lot #: W473	Complete W473
Thursday	etc.	
Friday	etc.	

This schedule could extend out into the following week, but normally not beyond that. Of course there would also be similar schedules for Line 2 and for all the other lines in this department.

Who develops the Finishing Schedule? Who has ownership? Usually it is *not* the Master Scheduler. Instead, it's often someone on the plant floor. It could be a person with a job title such as Plant Scheduler, Dispatcher, Foreman, Assistant Superintendent, and so forth. In our experience, it's good to have ownership of plant schedules with plant people, not someone in the office at headquarters.

One last point: It's important that the Master Schedule and the Finishing Schedule be coordinated and in sync. Regardless of who manages them, they need to be consistent with each other. Verifying this is a job for either the Master Scheduler or the Plant Scheduler or both, and it needs to be done frequently: once or several times per week.

Mixed Model Scheduling

Just-in-Time and Lean Manufacturing have triggered the emergence of Mixed Model Scheduling. Let's first see how it works and then we can talk about its benefits.

World Wide Widget's plant in Pennsylvania makes four types of medium widgets: models A, B, C, and D. The monthly production volume is around 200 units per month, ten per day. About 40 percent of that volume is in Model A, 30 percent in Model B, 20 percent in C, and 10 percent in D.

Prior to adopting Lean Manufacturing, the plant made each model once per month.

Day	1	2	3	4	5	6	7	8	9	10	11	12	13	14	15	16	17	18	19	20
Model:																				
A	10	10	10	10	10	10	10	10												
B									10	10	10	10	10	10						
C															10	10	10	10		
D																			10	10

Were there problems with this approach? Absolutely. And they were not insignificant:

• Inventory was higher than it needed to be, because they put a whole month's worth of a given model into stock at, effectively, the same time.

• Customer service was not as good as it should be. Sometimes there would be increased demand on a given model that would wipe out all the stock, but the plant wasn't scheduled to run that model again for another week or two. Sometimes Sales prevailed and the plant ran that model early. Sometimes the plant won, and the schedule wasn't changed.

These are two serious problems, so why did they do it that way? Answer: Changeovers were the villain. It took eight hours to change over the line from one model to another, an entire shift of unproductive time. The plant tried to avoid changeovers, or set-ups, whenever possible. Changeovers were a pain in the neck, and they made the plant's numbers look bad. (That's why the plant resisted making early changeovers in response to out-of-stock conditions.)

Once the plant learned about Lean Manufacturing — and its many benefits — they went to work on reducing changeover time. They succeeded, getting it down to eight minutes[4]. They could now economically run any model at just about any time. So they did.

The daily schedule, still at ten per day, looked like this:

Model A: 4

Model B: 3

Model C: 2

Model D: 1

Why do this? What did they accomplish? Well, they certainly improved the two problems we cited earlier: inventory and customer service. Inventories went down and customer service went up — *simultaneously* — and folks, it doesn't get any better than that. The inventories dropped because the production schedule matched much more closely how the product was sold: some of each product each week. Customer service went up because the plant was running each product every day — hence only one day away from availability.

There's another benefit, this one for the suppliers. Before Mixed Model, the suppliers had to ship components for Model A in Weeks 1 and 2, components for Model B in Weeks 2 and 3, and so forth. No more. Now each week, perhaps every day, the suppliers can ship the same mix of components.

One of the important concepts within Lean Manufacturing is that of *linearity*. Level the schedule; smooth things out; get rid of the lumps. When the suppliers know that each day and each week

---

4 Some of you may be thinking that this is pie-in-the-sky. Not so. Reducing set-up time from a number of hours to an equivalent number of minutes is not unusual, for companies that get serious about it. Frequently this is done with little or no additional capital investment. For more on this very important topic, see Shigeo Shingo's classic work: *A Revolution in Manufacturing: The SMED System*. Portland, OR: Productivity Press, 1985.

their production and shipping requirements will be the same, they'll be able to do a better job on cost, quality, and delivery.

Another important element within Lean Manufacturing is continuous improvement. At the World Wide plant, they continued to work on the changeover issue. Subsequently they cut changeover times down even further, to nearly zero. *Changeovers had become a non-issue.* They now were able to vary the sequence within a given day; the Finishing Schedule might look like this:

A   A   B   C   D   A   B   C   A   B

Why do this? Well, let's say that due to space constraints, the plant wants two deliveries per day: one for the first shift and one for the second. The suppliers would know that the first delivery would call for the first half of the schedule: two As, and one each of B, C, and D (AABCD). The second delivery would require components for the second half of the schedule: two As, two Bs, and one C (ABCAB).

One last point: Mixed Model Scheduling does not enable changeover reduction. It's the other way around: Sharply reduced set-up and changeover times enable Mixed Model Scheduling and its many attendant benefits. The moral of this story: Cut your changeover times very short before you attempt Mixed Model Scheduling.

Finite Scheduling Software

In the example several pages ago, the person who generated the plant schedule did so with a view towards two factors, one being when the jobs were needed and the other being the available capacity. Ignoring priorities runs the risk of making the wrong stuff. Disregarding the workload vs. capacity issue could readily result in overloading the resources, thus setting up an impossible task.

Good schedulers always keep both priority and capacity in mind. In most cases, they do so "manually," i.e., without substantial computer assistance. However, sometimes the task can be quite difficult, for example, where there are lots of products of varying work content and many different resources. Computer support for these complex scheduling tasks exists today. It goes under the generic name of Finite Scheduling software.

Finite Scheduling software, used intelligently and with accurate data, can be a big plus, particularly in complex environments. Let's take a look at one example.

<u>Mini Case: A Manufacturer of Injection Molded Plastic Products</u>. Company C has it's headquarters in Chicago and the largest of its four plants is in southern Indiana. Ellen, based in Chicago, is the Master Scheduler for all the plants. Gary is the Plant Scheduler at the Indiana plant; he and Ellen work together closely.

The environment at the plant is somewhat complex, with the following characteristics:

- The plant makes a wide variety of products.

- The customer base is broad and some customers are quite demanding, for example mass merchandisers.

- Speeds and volumes are high.

- There are over 40 injection molding machines, with varying capabilities.

- Proper sequencing of jobs on individual machines is important for efficiency purposes.

Ellen does an excellent job of maintaining the Master Schedule, using the standard tools described in this book, including Available-to-Promise. Her office is next to the Inside Sales department, which includes customer order entry. She is in frequent contact with those folks.

Twice per week, Gary at the plant downloads the Master Schedule from Ellen and fires up his Finite Scheduling program. He and the computer — working together interactively — develop the new schedule: firm for the next several days and tentative for the following week.

It's an iterative process. The computer assigns the jobs to specific work centers, taking care not to violate any Available-to-Promise commitments in the Master Schedule. While doing this, it keeps track of all of the relevant costs: inventory carrying costs, changeovers, stockouts, and so forth. It shows the schedule and each category of costs to Gary, who can override the computer's schedule and have the system try again.

For example, perhaps one day the computer-generated solution results in more stockouts than Gary feels are acceptable. He tells the system that. The Finite Scheduling software will reformulate the schedule, modify it, recalculate the costs, and display them again. If Gary doesn't like that solution, he overrides it and tells the system to try again. When he's happy with the schedule, he accepts it and that becomes what the plant runs.

This is an excellent example of using the power of the computer to simulate and perform massive amounts of calculations, while keeping control in the hands of the human being, who has product and process knowledge and who is *accountable* for the effectiveness of the schedules.

It goes without saying that these packages require large amounts of data to work really well. Data acquisition can be a big task during implementation. It may be worth it, though, because Finite Scheduling packages can be helpful, enabling people to generate better schedules with less effort. They are most useful in complex environments, less so in simpler ones.

Theory of Constraints

A popular concept in recent years is called the Theory of Constraints (TOC). Among other things, it states that the output of a plant is limited by its most severe constraint. The TOC says that an hour gained at a bottleneck resource is an hour gained for the entire factory; an hour gained at a non-bottleneck resource has little or no impact. In other words, optimize the performance of the constraint in order to get the most output from the plant. That makes sense to us.

Some of today's Finite Scheduling software claim to be based on the Theory of Constraints. Okay, that's fine. Most Finite Scheduling packages are built on avoiding loading more into a resource than it's capable of producing, which is what the TOC says also.

Master Scheduling for Outsourced Products

How does the Master Schedule work with products that the company does not produce, ones that are purchased complete from outside suppliers? Answer: about the same as it does for manufactured products. The only difference is that the Master Production Schedules are communicated directly to the suppliers — the "outside factories" — as opposed to one's own internal plants.

In Chapter 6, we saw a Master Schedule display for Product #11223, shown here as Figure 7-3. We've added one thing: the source, which is shown as purchased. (This is for information only; it has no effect on the Master Scheduling logic itself.)

The Master Production Schedules in Weeks 4 and 7 are shown as going directly to the supplier. Quite possibly there also would be other products sourced at this supplier; if so, they would be grouped

Figure 7-3

MASTER SCHEDULE DISPLAY — OUTSOURCED PRODUCTS

Product #11223   Lead Time = 1 week   Order Quantity = 25
                        Planning Time Fence @ Week 7   Source: Purchased
                                                       Supplier: F172

Week	PAST DUE	1	2	3	4	5	6	7	PTF 8
Sales Forecast		3	2	0	10	10	10	10	10
Customer Orders		7		18					
Total Demand		10	2	18	10	10	10	10	10
Projected Available Balance (OHB = 36)		26	24	6	21	11	1	16	6
Available-to-Promise		11			25			25	
Master Production Schedule (MPS)					**25F**			**25F**	

TO THE SUPPLIER

together in a (hopefully) coherent schedule, which would recognize the supplier's short-term capacity limits and not call for a level of production beyond them.

The supplier's ID number also is shown in this display, implying that this product is single sourced. In the case of multiple suppliers, each one could be listed along with the percentage of business allocated to each.

Finally, please note that we're showing no lead time offset for the MPSs. What's being communicated here is when the company wants these products to be completed and delivered, not when the supplier needs to start them into production. Good supplier scheduling processes typically work this way; they tell the supplier when they want the product and leave the internal lead time details up to the supplier.

Purchased Materials and Components

Okay, that sounds fine for finished products purchased from outside. But how about purchased materials and components? How does the Master Schedule send requirements for those items down the supply chain? Answer: It does so through either Material Requirements Planning (MRP), via Kanban signals, or a combination of both — plans via MRP and execution signals via Kanban.

In a conventional (read "non-Lean") environment, the Master Schedule sends its MPSs into Material Requirements Planning (MRP). MPSs in the Master Schedule are statements of supply, but become statements of demand as they're "exploded" via the bill of material into requirements for components and materials. It's MRP's job to collate all of the requirements for a given purchased item, net those requirements against that item's inventory and open order status, and calculate when more are needed and how many. That information is what's passed down the supply chain to the suppliers.

Here's why this happens within MRP rather than in the Master Schedule:

- MRP captures all of the requirements for a given item, using the bill of material. Let's say that one of the raw materials used to make Product #11223 is also used in several dozen other products. The logic of MRP is structured to determine the requirements of all of those products. The Master Schedule is usually not set up that way, because that's not its job.

- MRP knows the on-hand inventory balances of the purchased items; the Master Schedule does not.

- MRP knows the open order status of the purchased items; the Master Schedule does not.

- MRP knows the lead times, lot sizing rules, safety stock requirements, and so forth for the purchased items; the Master Schedule does not.

For more on this topic, including a discussion of the process known as Supplier Scheduling, please see John Schorr's *Purchasing in the 21st Century*, second edition, New York: John Wiley & Sons, 1998.

Reconciliation — Master Production Schedule to Aggregate Production Plan

The sales forecast is a statement of expected future demand. As we said back in Chapter 4, the detailed forecast needs to match the aggregate; there must be a process in place to do that.

Similarly, on the supply side, the details need to match the aggregate. The sum of the Master Production Schedules for a given product family or group needs to closely match the aggregate Production Plan authorized by top management in the Executive S&OP process.

Figure 7-4 indicates a problem in the first month, with the sum of the MPS exceeding the Production Plan by a sizeable margin. What needs to take place here is either:

• a reduction in the quantity of MPSs in the first month to match the Production Plan, or

• an authorization from top management to raise the Production Plan to match the MPSs, or

• some combination thereof, to get these two sets of plans in sync.

Figure 7-4

RECONCILIATION — MPSs to PRODUCTION PLAN
LARGE INDUSTRIAL WIDGETS
PLANNING TIME FENCE = 8 WEEKS

Week	1	2	3	4	Month 1	5	6	7	8	Month 2
PRODUCTION PLAN (from Exec S&OP)					**100**					**100**
Master Production Schedules:										
L1	20			40	60	10		10	20	40
L2		20	10		30	10	10	10	10	40
L3	10		10	20	<u>40</u>		20			<u>20</u>
TOTALS					**130**					**100**
DIFFERENCE					**+30**					

To sum up, it's the Master Production Schedules that directly drive plant and supplier activity, not the Production Plan. Without this check, there is no assurance that the plants and suppliers are marching to the right drummer. Top management needs the assurance that their decisions, in this case regarding the level of production, are being carried out.

Chapter 8

SUPPORTING THE STRATEGIES: PART 1 — BUILDING TO STOCK

Back in Chapter 2, we discussed the question: Where do you meet the customer? We said that this refers to that point where the customer order is received, and that it has a major impact on how Master Scheduling is done. We referred to the different choices, shown here in Figure 8-1, as Order Fulfillment Strategies.

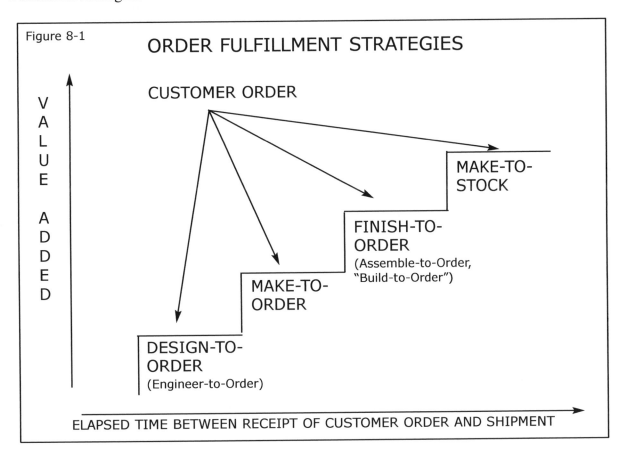

Figure 8-1   ORDER FULFILLMENT STRATEGIES

So the question arises: Specifically, how does Master Scheduling support the various Order Fulfillment Strategies? Getting into that issue is the purpose of both this chapter and the next.

Make-to-Stock Defined

We've seen a number of examples of simple Make-to-Stock Master Schedules, so there's no need to repeat one here. However, this might be a good place to talk about what is, and what isn't, a Make-to-Stock product. Some people feel that, if they make a product specifically for one customer,   then it's Make-to-Order. For example, Company BW makes buggy whips and one of their models, Product #234, is sold exclusively to LargeMart, a mass merchandiser.

LargeMart requires that they keep a minimum of two weeks of inventory in their warehouse to protect against stockouts. As far as how Master Scheduling will treat this item, it's Make-to-Stock; there's a finished goods inventory, and the Projected Available Balance row will be a very important factor in setting the timing of the Master Production Schedules. So the issue of Make-to-Stock or Make-to-Order is not does only one customer buy the product; rather, it's whether the product moves through a finished goods inventory.

Supporting Multiple Distribution Centers

Some companies ship their products from more than one location, perhaps from a network of distribution centers (DCs) or branch warehouses. They do this for a variety of reasons. One is their customers' perceived needs for availability; the customers want access to the product very quickly. Another important issue can be freight costs: Shipping less-than-truckload quantities over long distances might be considered cost prohibitive for some products.

During the last twenty years or so, however, there's been a significant reduction in the use of stocking/shipping points. A number of factors have contributed to this:

- More flexible manufacturing, including shorter lead times and mixed model scheduling

- More rapid freight delivery by common carriers thanks to air freight, deregulation, and other factors

- Faster access to information

- A heightened awareness of the costs and difficulty involved in storing inventory

- Greater understanding that spreading inventory among more stocking points makes the demand more lumpy and thus less linear, necessitating more safety stock and higher inventories

We know of companies that have cut back on the number of their DCs substantially, on the theory that faster freight can lead to fewer shipping points. Others have eliminated DCs completely. They've decided that the costs of staffing, maintaining, and operating DCs — along with the costs of carrying more inventory — are greater than the increased costs of rapid transportation to customers over longer distances.

Given all that, the fact still remains that many companies ship their products to their customers from more than one DC. So the question arises: How does this impact Master Scheduling? Well, if the Master Schedule's role is to balance demand and supply, then it must see *all* the demand — not only customer demand but also demand for the replenishment of the DCs.

It's time for a quiz. Here are the parameters:

- Product #56395 is shipped to customers from the plant in Indianapolis.

- The plant also replenishes the inventory of #56395 at the Los Angeles Distribution Center.

- Two-thirds of the volume is shipped to customers from Indy; one-third from L.A.

- The nationwide sales rate is 60 units per week and stable; we can assume the forecast error is quite low.

True or false: The future demand in the Master Schedule should look like this?

Week	1	2	3	4	5	6	7	8
Forecast	60	60	60	60	60	60	60	60

The answer is false. The demand is not going to occur like that. It's true that Indianapolis's demand from customers will be reasonably linear, and so will L.A.'s. But — and here's the key point — Indianapolis is not shipping to L.A.'s *customers*; it' shipping to the L.A. Distribution Center. It does this via rail cars, once per month. The demand here is not linear; it's lumpy. So here's how the demand really should look for the Master Schedule at the Indy plant:

Week	1	2	3	4	5	6	7	8
Forecast (Indy)	40	40	40	40	40	40	40	40
DC Demand — L.A.		80				80		
TOTAL DEMAND	40	120	40	40	40	120	40	40

Putting these demand numbers into our standard Master Schedule format results in the Master Schedule display shown in Figure 8-2. (For clarity, we've removed the rows for Customer Demand and Available-to-Promise; in a real world display, those rows would be present as would some safety stock or safety time.)

Figure 8-2

MASTER SCHEDULE DISPLAY — DISTRIBUTION CENTER DEMAND

Product #56395

Week	PAST DUE	1	2	3	4	5	6	7	8
Sales Forecast		40	40	40	40	40	40	40	40
DC Demand — L.A.			80				80		
Total Demand		40	120	40	40	40	120	40	40
Projected Available Balance (OHB = 140)		100	60	20	60	20	60	20	60
Master Production Schedule (MPS)			80F		80F		160F		80F

We'd like to call your attention to the Master Production Schedule in Week 2. If we had been using an average demand of 60 per week, the first MPS would logically appear in Week 3, not Week 2. Let's try it:

Week	1	2	3	4	5	6	7	8
Total Demand	60	60	60	60	60	60	60	60
Projected Balance (OHB = 140)	80	20	20					

The logic of Master Scheduling would have called for a replenishment order in Week 3, because Week 2 still has a positive balance. Or, if the Master Production Schedule was already in Week 2, the logic would have generated a reschedule out recommendation, as shown on the next page.

Week	1	2	3	4	5	6	7	8
Total Demand	60	60	60	60	60	60	60	60
Projected Balance (OHB = 140)	80	100	40					
Master Production Schedule (MPS)		80F →						

Action message: Reschedule MPS Week 2 to Week 3

Of course this is erroneous, because the true demand is 40 in Week 1 and 120 in Week 2, as we saw earlier. If the MPS were rescheduled out, this would probably cause a shortage when the monthly order for L.A. is pulled for shipment.

It rarely works well to use a nationwide forecast when shipping from remote points, because the demand that the Master Schedule needs to see is not when will the remote locations ship to customers; rather, it's when will the remote locations be replenished? Thus:

> **Principle #13: The Master Schedule must see the true demand.**
> **When remote stocking points exist, their demand is dependent**
> **upon how those remote points will be replenished.**

Heightening this need for seeing the true demand is the fact that most distribution networks contain more than one DC. In our simple example, we had a plant in Indianapolis and a DC in Los Angeles. A more typical network might look like that shown in Figure 8-3.

Distribution Requirements Planning

In replenishing distribution centers, the tool of choice for many companies is Distribution Requirements Planning (DRP)[1]. It employs much of the same logic that we've seen for Master Scheduling: time-phasing, gross-to-net calculations, lead time offset, and so on. DRP calculates the replenishment schedule based on the demand-supply picture for each product at each DC.

---

[1] For a full discussion of DRP, we recommend Andre Martin's book: *Distribution Resource Planning*, New York: John Wiley & Sons, (1995).

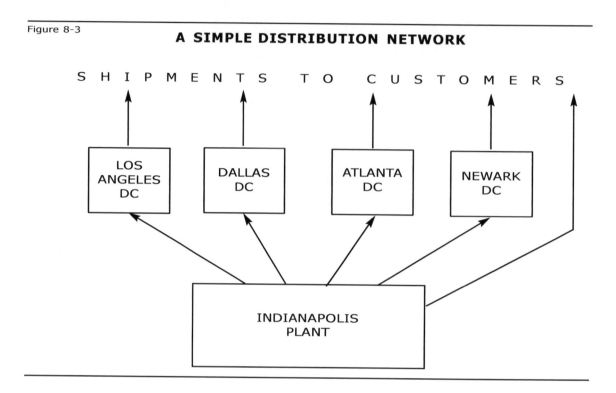

Figure 8-3

A SIMPLE DISTRIBUTION NETWORK

Let's look at a sample DRP display for the stockkeeping unit we've been working with: Product #56395 at the L.A. Distribution Center, shown in Figure 8-4. Let's take it from the top:

• The lead time of one week refers to the time involved in pulling the order at Indianapolis, getting it to Los Angeles, and receiving it at the DC.

• The order quantity of 80 may represent a container, or perhaps a full truckload.

• The safety stock of 20 represents a one-week supply, to protect against uncertainty of demand — or possibly against uncertainty of supply, if the freight arrangements are not highly reliable.

• Speaking of uncertainty of demand, the sales forecast is for 20 per week. Will the orders come in at exactly 20 per week? Of course not. That's why safety stock is frequently employed in cases like these.

• The replenishment orders, offset for one week of lead time, are passed to the Master Schedule. You may want to refer back to Figure 8-2 and check the second row in the display, labeled DC Demand — L.A. There are the 80 in Week 2 and 80 in Week 6. Those replenishment orders drive the logic of Master Scheduling to have availability to cover them.

Figure 8-4

DRP DISPLAY — LOS ANGELES DISTRIBUTION CENTER

Product #56395   Replenishment Lead Time = 1 week   Order Quantity = 80
Safety Stock = 20

Week	PAST DUE	1	2	3	4	5	6	7	8
Sales Forecast		20	20	20	20	20	20	20	20
Projected Available Balance (OHB = 65)		45	25	85	65	45	25	85	65
Replenishment Orders at Receipt				80				80	
Replenishment Orders at Shipment		80					80		

TO   MASTER SCHEDULE

Is DRP the only way to do this? No. Is it the best way to do it? Yes and no. In environments of moderate or greater complexity, the answer is almost always yes. But when things are simpler, with short lead times, daily or weekly replenishment cycles, little or no seasonality, low freight costs, then DRP might not be worth the effort. A leaner, less elaborate approach — Kanban perhaps — might be a better choice.

DRP, in order to work well, requires highly accurate inventory records and detailed forecasts by product by distribution center. This latter requirement, forecasts by DC, leads some companies to work on simplifying their environment rather than investing time, effort, and money into what might be a huge forecasting job. (A company with 5,000 finished products — not a large number in many industries — that stocks all of them in 10 DCs would be required to make forecasts for 50,000 SKUs, and that's a bunch.)

At the end of the day, valid DC demand needs to enter the Master Schedule so that the product can be planned for and shipped. In companies with moderate to high complexity in the upper end of their supply chain, DRP is normally the best way to do that.

Vendor Managed Inventories

Let's assume for a moment that the Los Angeles Distribution Center is not owned by the company itself but is a public warehouse. Need it be treated any differently with regard to planning and scheduling? Not at all. The same approach (DRP or whatever) can be used, with the resultant replenishment orders being passed down as demand into the Master Schedule.

What if that DC in Los Angeles were not a public warehouse but rather owned by a customer? Need this customer DC be treated any differently than a company would treat its own DC or a public one? Probably not, particularly if an approach called Vendor Managed Inventories (VMI) is utilized.

VMI calls for a close working relationship between the customer and supplier, and places the replenishment decision-making in the hands of the supplier. In effect, the customer is saying to the supplier: "You keep me in stock. Don't let me run out. And oh by the way, don't load me up with lots of unneeded inventory[2]."

It's then the supplier's job to do just that. In order for that to happen consistently — in stock without excessive inventories — the supplier's Master Schedule must have good visibility into those demands. It's the Master Schedule that specifies which products are built at what times and in which quantities. It can't do that well unless it can see *all* the demands, as they're expected to happen.

Efficient Consumer Response, Quick Response, and Collaborative Planning Forecasting & Replenishment

We'd like to address these items together, because the similarities among them are greater than the differences. The terminology here is a bit crowded: Efficient Consumer Response (ECR) is used primarily in the grocery industry while Quick Response (QR) is seen more often general merchandise environments[3].

---

[2] In some cases, the customers own the inventory at their location; in others it's on consignment. In either case, it's in the best interest of both parties not to have the inventories higher than what's needed.

[3] Another term with a somewhat similar meaning is Continuous Replenishment. Efficient Replenishment is used here also, and it is a subset of Efficient Consumer Response.

In this book, we've talked quite a bit about Supply Chain Management and also about Lean Manufacturing. Well, one way to think of ECR/QR is that it's a Lean Manufacturing approach applied across the supply chain — both up and down — involving retailers, wholesalers, and the manufacturers who supply them.

ECR /QR is a strategy, a methodology, and a set of processes in which manufacturers, distributors, and retailers work very closely together to provide increased value to the consumer. It focuses on the efficiency of the *total* supply chain, rather than sub-optimizing one or another component of it.

This approach is based on ground-breaking work done primarily at Wal-Mart during the 1980s. That company has had an enormous impact on how retailers and manufacturers work together. *Wal-Mart is to retailing as the Japanese have been to manufacturing: They have thrown away the old rule book and have written a brand new one.* Retailing, for retail stores and for the manufacturing companies that supply them, is becoming a whole new ball game.

What about Collaborative Planning, Forecasting, and Replenishment (CPFR)? Well, CPFR is much newer than ECR/QR and is actually an outgrowth of it. Dr. Dirk Siefert of the Harvard Business School states: " . . . CPFR is considered a further development of Efficient Consumer Response on the supply side. The intensified efforts in cooperative supply chain management like Cross Docking, Vendor Managed Inventories (VMI) and Continuous Replenishment in evidence since the early nineties find in CPFR a further development of collaboration[4]."

ECR/QR and CPFR raise the high bar dramatically for manufacturers. They call for, among other things, a high degree of flexibility. For example, ECR/QR won't work well in a plant that makes extended production runs of one product to compensate for long changeover times. Let's look at one manufacturer's experience and, as we do, note how the role of the Master Scheduler changed during the transition.

Mini Case: A Producer of Consumer Packaged Goods

Company K produces a wide range of consumer products, distributed through a variety of retail companies, including mass merchandisers. Early on, they had a very narrow product line, which became highly successful, commanding a 90 percent market share. This credibility gave them the opportunity over the last ten years to grow their business into additional consumer products, expanding the number of stockkeeping units by a large multiple.

---

4 Dirk Siefert, *Collaborative Planning, Forecasting and Replenishment*, (2002), Bonn, Germany: Galileo Press, p. 39.

Their two plants contained filling lines that placed liquid or paste products into containers. Some of these containers had very long purchasing lead times, caused by complex graphics designed to attract consumers' attention in the retail store. The product was mixed in large batches and then fed to a number of filling lines that would run a given SKU for many days on end. These long runs of course were due to long changeover times.

The resulting large quantities of product were sent to a central warehouse, from which they shipped to dozens of customer Distribution Centers (DCs), located geographically from coast to coast and all over the world. One Master Scheduler served both plants. Based on specific customer DC schedules and market forecasts by SKU, the Master Scheduler developed plant schedules for production and shipments to customers. As the number of SKUs expanded over the years, the Master Scheduling tasks became more and more difficult to keep up with.

One day, things began to change. It started with one of their largest customer's adoption of Quick Response. This customer informed them that they were going to eliminate the scheduling and shipping of product to DCs. Rather, they would require Company K to ship directly to over 2000 stores at least once per week. The customer indicated they would provide Company K with daily downloads of their point of sale data, as scanned at the cash register. With this data, Company K was expected to keep thousands of retail shelves full.

After an initial effort to talk the customer out of doing this, the scramble was on — how was Company K to handle this fundamental change to their business? The following tasks were identified as necessary:

- Organize the daily download of yesterday's sales in such a way as to see loads by line and merge them with schedules from other customers, assuring that they are in accordance with the Production Plan authorized in Executive S&OP.

- Reorganize packing and shipping to handle small shipments, right off the line.

- Establish finished goods Kanbans (see Appendix F) to trigger visual replenishment of high-volume SKUs with uniform demand.

- Create line flexibility so that lot sizes can be reduced without excessive changeover time and costs.

- Redesign and develop more standard packaging materials (with some of the unique marking done in-line) to reduce long purchasing lead time and increase responsiveness.

Company K implemented all these changes. As they took hold, a new vision became clear. If they were to succeed in this new world of Efficient Consumer Response, they would have to learn how to cost-effectively accomplish the following:

YESTERDAY'S POINT-OF-SALE DEMAND IS

TONIGHT'S PRODUCTION AND

TOMORROW'S SHIPMENTS.

This became their rallying cry. With a lot of hard work, they got there and it revolutionized how they ran their business. One of the many things that changed: The role of the Master Scheduler needed to expand from detailed scheduling and decision making to one of policy development, implementation, and monitoring. See Figure 8-5 for a comparison.

Company K recognized that while the Master Scheduler's role was very different, it was no less (and perhaps more) important than before. In Chapter 10, we'll revisit the changing role of the Master Scheduler.

Figure 8-5

Changes in the Master Scheduler's Job at Company K

Old Job

- Create firm Master Production Schedule from planned orders at the Planning Time Fence.

- Release MPSs to the plants.

- Respond to exception messages, coordinating change.

- Coordinate plant filling schedules.

- Resolve conflict between plant efficiency and customer needs.

- Schedule shipments to customers.

New Job

- Monitor daily download of customer sales data that is directly scheduling the plants.

- Monitor Finished Goods Kanbans for those selected high-volume SKUs used for load leveling.

- Work with customers and design people to standardize product to further enable high response and cost effectiveness.

- Play a significant support role in the Executive S&OP process.

- Continue to do those relatively few parts of the "old job" that still remain.

Chapter 9

SUPPORTING THE STRATEGIES: PART 2 — BUILDING TO CUSTOMER ORDER

Let's revisit our "where do we meet the customer" diagram, shown here as Figure 9-1. Here we can see the three "to-order" strategies: finish-to-order, make-to-order, and design-to-order.

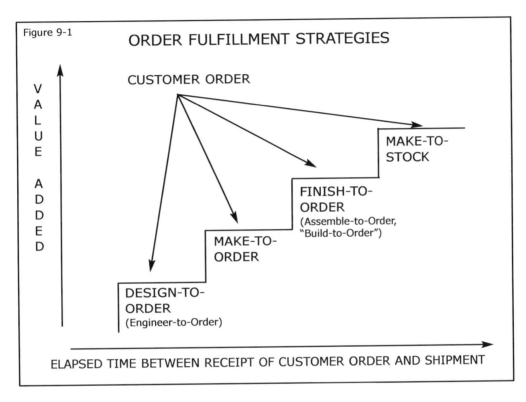

Producing products to customer order is quite a bit different from making to stock. To do it well, we need to understand the concept of order backlog.

The customer order backlog contains not just orders that are past due, but all of the unshipped customer orders in house, irrespective of when they're due to be shipped. An order due to ship six months from now is as much a part of the backlog as one that was due to ship last week but is not yet finished.

Why would some companies want to have order backlogs? Well, some don't; they're called make-to-stock. On the other hand, companies building to customer order will have some degree of backlog, perhaps as short as a few hours up to a number of months and in some cases, even years. The reason there must be some degree of backlog in these companies is that they don't finish making the product until after they get the order. It takes them a certain amount of time to do so and that amount of time largely determines the minimum size of the backlog.

Let's ask ourselves: Would a company that's good at Lean Manufacturing tend to have a shorter or longer backlog than one not doing Lean? Obviously, the answer is shorter. That's a major contribution made by Lean Manufacturing and Just-in-Time over the past quarter century: more efficient production, leading to shorter lead times, enabling smaller order backlogs.

Companies building to customer order typically see three distinct time zones for the backlog:

1. The Sold Zone — contains only sold orders

2. The Partially Sold Zone — contains some sold orders and some forecast

3. The Unsold Zone — contains only forecast

In Figure 9-2 we can see this depicted graphically. Keep this in mind as we go forward because it has relevance to almost any kind of environment where products are made to customer order.

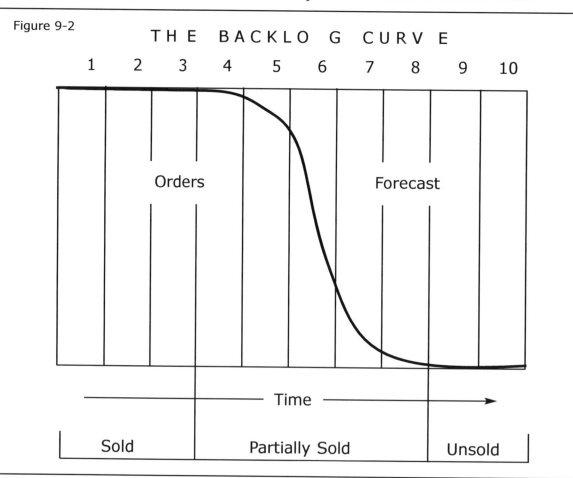

Figure 9-2

THE BACKLOG CURVE

Supporting Finish-to-Order
(Assemble-to-Order, Build-to-Order[1])

Back in Chapter 2, we cited two factors that are very important for an effective finish-to-order process, one being an understanding and acceptance of the concept of postponement and the other being Planning Bills of Material.

Postponement refers to not adding the options to the product until *after* the customer order is received. Let's say we're making wagons that come in three different colors: red, white, and blue. Postponement would tell us to build the wagons ahead of time, but not to paint them until the customer orders arrive. Then finish them — paint, package, and ship — very quickly.

Planning Bills of Material

The other element usually needed for finish-to-order is planning bills of material[2]. First, let's dissect this phrase. "Planning" means that this is a technique used in future planning. The term "bills of material"[3] refers to a grouping of the components necessary to make a product. However — and here's the tricky part — planning bills are not producible; you normally can't make anything directly from a planning bill. They exist solely for *planning* purposes, so that material and capacity can be available when the customer order arrives.

The World Wide Widget Company manufactures widgets for home and industry, and one of their product families is called Small Consumer Widgets. Each product in this family contains a base unit, a control module, a power supply, a sensor, and packaging. The base unit is standard across all models in this family, while the other components vary from product to product, as follows:

Control Module	5 options
Sensor	4 options
Power Supply	3 options
Packaging	20 variations (depending on product configuration, private brand customer, and so on)
Base Unit	standard

---

[1] "Mass Customization" is another term frequently used in this context.

[2] This material was adapted from *Sales Forecasting: A New Approach.*

[3] Other terms for bills of material include formulas, recipes, or ingredients list.

Figure 9-3 shows this arrangement graphically.

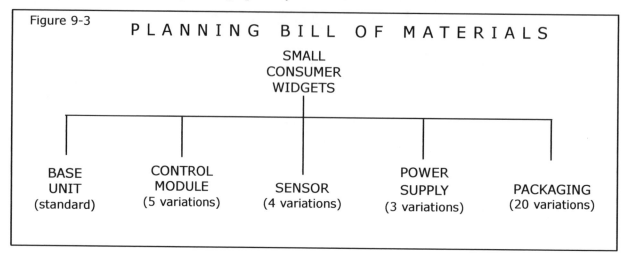

Figure 9-3

PLANNING BILL OF MATERIALS

SMALL CONSUMER WIDGETS

BASE UNIT (standard) — CONTROL MODULE (5 variations) — SENSOR (4 variations) — POWER SUPPLY (3 variations) — PACKAGING (20 variations)

Given this array of options, the theoretically possible number of models within small consumer widgets is 1,200 (5 control modules *times* 4 sensors *times* 3 power supplies *times* 20 packaging variations *times* 1 base unit). This means potentially 1,200 end items to forecast. This will be particularly challenging when one considers that the annual sales for this entire product family are about 8,500 units per month (less than 8 per possible model). The law of large numbers is definitely not at work here.

World Wide should consider setting up a modular planning bill for this product family. This is an arrangement that will show each option and its projected frequency of being ordered by customers. In Figure 9-4, we can see that the base unit has a forecasted frequency of 100 percent. This makes sense, because there is only one base unit; it's standard and every customer order for small consumer widgets will need one of them.

On the other hand, the five control module options are shown along with their forecasted frequency of order, expressed as a percentage. Ditto for the other options. Keep in mind that these percentages are truly forecasts, i.e., projections of customer orders for these optional items. Most companies derive these primarily from past history, with adjustments for new options, changing customer preferences, pricing, and so forth.

So, if World Wide were to use a planning bill, how many possible end items would they need to forecast and Master Schedule? Answer: only 34 (5 control modules *plus* 4 sensors *plus* 3 power

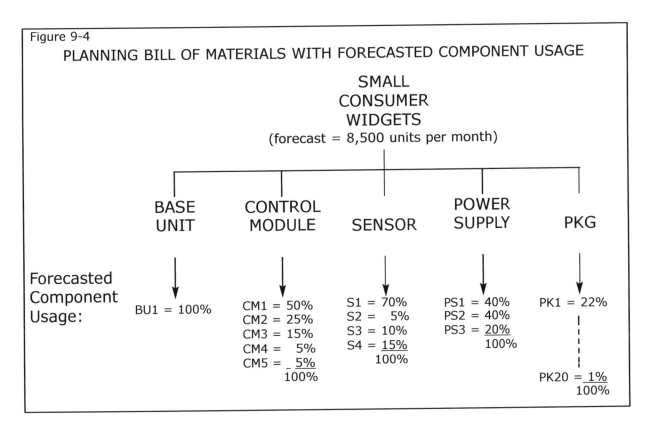

Figure 9-4

PLANNING BILL OF MATERIALS WITH FORECASTED COMPONENT USAGE

supplies *plus* 20 packaging variations *plus* 1 base unit[4] *plus* one more that we'll talk about in the next paragraph). Thirty-four is a far cry from 1,200. This will take advantage of the law of large numbers, thus making forecasting easier and, at the same time, sharply reducing forecast error. Better results for less effort.

Two-Level Master Schedule

In a finish-to-order environment, what actually gets Master Scheduled? Well, certainly all the options, including the common parts. But there is often another item in the Master Schedule, one representing the product family itself, that "sits on top" of the modules similarly to what we've just seen in Figure 9-4 for the Small Consumer Widgets family.

---

[4] In actual practice, companies often take all of the common parts from the option components and group them together into what's called a "common parts bill." For example, let's say every sensor option uses the same housing. That housing could be pulled from the sensor bills of material and placed with the base unit, carrying a usage of 100 percent. Common parts bills help to reduce uncertainty, risk, and inventories, at the cost of some added complexity.

Companies using Executive S&OP (see Appendix A) would develop an aggregate sales forecast and production plan for this family in monthly time buckets for many months into the future. The near term portion of that plan would be "chopped up" into weeks and would look similar to Figure 9-5, which shows a Master Schedule display for the Small Consumer Widget family and one of its options.

Please note several things about the upper half of the display, which deals with the family:

- The sales forecast is shown in weekly increments, 12 per week. Ditto for the Master Schedule.

- The backlog curve can be seen at work here: Weeks 1 through 3 contain customer orders only (Sold zone); Weeks 4 though 6 are a mix of orders and forecast (Partial zone); and beyond that there is only forecast (Forecast zone).

- The Available-to-Promise is being calculated normally, exactly as we've seen earlier. This ATP directly supports the promising of orders for Small Consumer Widgets *in general* and also makes it possible to check for the *specific options* called out on individual customer orders.

Let's expand on that for a moment. Let's say a customer is on the phone ready to place an order for eight Small Consumer Widgets in Week 5. Will we be able to meet that order?

If you said yes, you might have jumped the gun. While it's true that we have availability for eight Small Consumer Widgets *in general*, we won't know if we can meet the order until we check *each of the options that this specific order is requesting.*

In addition to other options, this particular order requires Control Module 1. Looking at the ATP for that option (the lower half of Figure 9-5), we can see that we have only five available through Week 5. Thus, as things stand now, we can't commit to that order. We'll have to get creative and see what might be done to meet the customer's need. Maybe we can reschedule some CM1s in from a later period, "borrowing" capacity and components from another module. The order should be promised only after confirming availability on all of the options requested.

Several other things to notice about the display for CM1 in Figure 9-5:

- The Sales Forecast row is blank. This means that there is no *independent* demand[5] for this item; apparently it is not sold directly to customers for service or repair.

---

[5] Independent demand comes from outside the company, from customers. Dependent demand *depends* on an upstream production plan or schedule.

Figure 9-5

MASTER SCHEDULE DISPLAY
SMALL CONSUMER WIDGET PRODUCT FAMILY AND CONTROL MODULE 1 OPTION

Product SCW SMALL CONSUMER WIDGETS — Lead Time = 1 week, Planning Time Fence @ Week 6, Demand Time Fence @ Week 3 — Order Quantity = 1 FOR 1

Week	PAST DUE	1	2	3	4	5	6	7	8
Sales Forecast					2	6	8	12	12
Customer Orders		12	12	12	10	6	4		
Total Demand		12	12	12	12	12	12	12	12
Projected Available Balance (OHB = 0)		0	0	0	0	0	0	0	0
Available-to-Promise — Period					2	6	8	12	12
Available-to-Promise — Cumulative					2	8	16	28	40
MPS		12R	12F	12F	12F	12F	12F	12	12

Product CM1 CONTROL MODULE 1 (50% option) — Lead Time = 1 week, Planning Time Fence @ Week 6, Demand Time Fence @ Week 3 — Order Quantity = 1 FOR 1

Week	PAST DUE	1	2	3	4	5	6	7	8
Sales Forecast									
Production Forecast					1	3	4	6	6
Customer Orders		5	7	9	6	2	2		
Total Demand		5	7	9	7	5	6	6	6
Projected Available Balance (OHB = 0)		1	0	1	0	1	1	1	1
Available-to-Promise — Period				1		4	4	6	6
Available-to-Promise — Cumulative				1	1	5	9	15	21
MPS		6R	6F	10F	6F	6F	6F	6	6

- The Production Forecast row contains future forecast, but it's *dependent* demand; it's derived directly from the parent item: the Small Consumer Widget family.

- All of the MPSs for CM1 call for a quantity of 6 except the one in Week 3, which is 10.

Let's get into more detail on these last two items: the Production Forecast and the unusual MPS in Week 3.

The Production Forecast

In the Production Forecast row, where did those numbers come from and why?

They came from the parent. They're the result of taking SCW's Available-to-Promise quantities and multiplying them by the quantity in the Planning Bill of Material[6]. For example, the ATP for the parent item in Week 4 is 2, multiplied by .5, gives 1, which is the quantity in CM1's Production Forecast for Week 4. Similar calculations are there for Weeks 5 through 8.

Second question: why? Let's look at SCW, the parent, in Week 4. We have sold customer orders for 10 that week, with 2 remaining in the Sales Forecast. The orders for 10 tell us *exactly* which options the customers are asking for; there is no uncertainty. In this example, of the 10 SCMs ordered in Week 4, 6 of them are specifying Control Module 1.

How do we know that? Simply by looking at the Customer Orders row in CM1. In Week 4, there's a quantity of 6.That represents the number of CM1s on the 10 orders for Small Consumer Widgets in Week 4. It's a fact.

The only uncertainty remaining in Week 4 is with what hasn't been sold, and that information is contained in the Available-to-Promise. In our example, the period ATP for Small Consumer Widgets in Week 4 is 2. Fifty percent of two is one and that's the Production Forecast for the module shown in Week 4.

One last point: You may have noticed that, for the parent item (SCW), the Sales Forecast and the Available-to-Promise are the same. This reflects the fact that both the Sales Forecast and the MPSs are set at 12 per week, as they quite possibly would be in a Lean Manufacturing environment. If the

---

[6] This is not the only workable method for determining the Production Forecast. It is, however, the simplest and it is the one we recommend.

MPSs were in larger lumps, say 36 every three weeks, then the period ATP would look quite different as would the Production Forecast for Control Module 1. Please see Figure 9-6. Now it's easy to see the differences between the Sales Forecast and Available-to-Promise.

Hedging

Let's take another look at the MPSs for Control Module 1. Why is the MPS in Week 3 for 10, when all the other MPSs are for 6? It's quite fortunate that the Week 3 MPS is for 10, because otherwise we would not be able to promise all these orders. What's going on?

Figure 9-6

MASTER SCHEDULE DISPLAY
SMALL CONSUMER WIDGET PRODUCT FAMILY WITH LARGER MPS ORDER QUANTITIES

Product SCW — SMALL CONSUMER WIDGETS

Lead Time = 1 week
Planning Time Fence @ Week 6
Demand Time Fence @ Week 3

Order Quantity = 3 Weeks Supply

Week	PAST DUE	1	2	3	4	5	6	7	8
Sales Forecast					2	6	8	12	12
Customer Orders		12	12	12	10	6	4		
Total Demand		12	12	12	12	12	12	12	12
Projected Available Balance (OHB = 0)		24	12	0	2	12	0	24	12
Available-to-Promise — Period					**16**		**36**		
MPS	36R				36F		36		
To Production Forecast for CM1					**8**		**18**		

To understand what's happening, let's look once more at the Control Module options for this product family, which we first saw in Figure 9-4:

$$CM1 = 50\%$$
$$CM2 = 25\%$$
$$CM3 = 15\%$$
$$CM4 = 5\%$$
$$CM5 = \underline{\ 5\%}$$
$$100\%$$

The percentages are the forecasts of anticipated demand coming in on customer orders. We're forecasting that half of the orders will call for CM1, 25 percent for CM2, and so on. The Master Schedule for CM1, shown in Figure 9-5, reflects that 50 percent forecast.

Well, what's the one sure thing about forecasts? They'll be wrong. If we plan to have *exactly* 50 percent availability of CM1s, 25 percent of CM2s, and so forth, we're not going to be able to cover the customer demand because the orders won't come in exactly as forecasted. Hence the need for hedging, or overplanning the options.

Now the way *not* to do this is to simply raise the percentages: Make CM1 55 percent, CM2 30 percent, and so on. This is not a good idea because it will tend to cause higher levels of planning, production, and procurement *out across the entire horizon* of the Master Schedule. That can be expensive — and unnecessary — protection. (It can also damage the credibility of the Master Schedule when people recognize that this deliberate overplanning is a way of life.)

Instead, the way to get protection effectively and economically is to use what's called a rolling mix hedge. Let's examine each word, starting with the last:

- It's a *hedge* against uncertainty.

- It addresses the uncertainty of the option *mix*, not the overall volume of the family itself. (A hedge on the family item, or preferably on the common parts bill, would be a volume hedge.)

- It's not static, but rather it's *rolled* by the Master Scheduler — in or out depending on whether demand is higher or lower than forecasted.

Let's look again at the MPSs for Control Module 1:

Week	PAST DUE	1	2	3	4	5	6	7	8
MPS		6F	6F	10F	6F	6F	6F	6F	6F

The hedge quantity is 4 and it's in Week 3. Why? Because that's where it's needed. Looking back at Figure 9-5, we can see that the Control Module has sold above forecast in the first three weeks, the Sold Zone. The Customer Order row shows sales of 5 + 7 + 9 for a total of 21 against a forecast of 18 (6 per week).

If the hedge hadn't been there, the company would have been hard pressed to promise and deliver all 21 units ordered in the first three weeks.

So what happens to the hedge when the orders are below forecast? In that case, the hedge should be rolled out a bit. Let's check Figure 9-7, which shows the CM1 Module with fewer orders in the Sold Zone; instead of 21 there are only 15 against a forecast of 18 for that three-week period. The hedge

Figure 9-7

MASTER SCHEDULE DISPLAY — CONTROL MODULE 1 OPTION

Product CM1
CONTROL MODULE 1

Lead Time = 1 week
Planning Time Fence @ Week 6
Demand Time Fence @ Week 3

Order Quantity = 1 FOR 1

Week	PAST DUE	1	2	3	4	5	6	7	8
Sales Forecast									
Production Forecast					1	3	4	6	6
Customer Orders		**5**	**4**	**6**	6	2	2		
Total Demand		5	4	6	7	5	6	6	6
Projected Available Balance (OHB = 0)		1	3	3	2	7	7	7	7
Available-to-Promise — Period		1	2			8	4	6	6
Available-to-Promise — Cumulative		1	3	3	3	11	15	21	27
MPS		6R	6F	6F	6F	**10F**	6F	6	6

quantity of 4 has been rolled out to Week 5. There's no additional production needed earlier: The Sold Zone is a done deal and we have a Production Forecast of only 1 in Week 4. Therefore, the first real exposure to uncertainty begins to occur in Week 5, where we have a Production Forecast of 3. This is a result of multiplying the ATP of the Small Consumer Widget family, which is 6, times the quantity in the Planning Bill of 0.5. So our forecast is for 3 in Week 5, but for product family SCW, we may sell as many as 6 additional units along with the 2 we've already booked, for a total of 8. If all of those orders were to specify CM1, then without the hedge, we couldn't cover that. That's why the hedge is in Week 5.

Normally the hedge sits early in the Partial Zone, the area that contains a mix of sold orders and forecast. In our first CM1 example, the hedge was in the Sold Zone, reflecting the higher than normal bookings for the first three weeks. Perhaps the Master Scheduler moved it in when s/he saw the order pattern developing.

Why is the hedge quantity 4? Well, setting hedge quantities is a rather inexact science; frequently the process used does not involve higher mathematics but rather "Kentucky windage." In our example, the hedge of 4 represents between one half and one full week's coverage which may, in the Master Scheduler's opinion and experience, provide sufficient protection at a reasonable cost.

To sum up our discussion on hedging and option overplanning:

- If you're going to be in the finish-to-order business, and use modular planning bills, you will need to do some kind of option overplanning.

- The option percentages are forecasts, and thus they will almost always be wrong.

- Inflating the option percentages causes overplanning across the entire horizon; it is inefficient, expensive, and can damage the credibility of the Master Schedule.

- Hedging is a proven method that is effective, efficient, and normally not expensive. It is the tool of choice to provide protection for option percentage forecast error.

The Finishing Schedule

You may be wondering how anything gets built, because you sure can't build the planning bill. Remember though, that when the customer order arrives, there is certainty as to what is needed. At that point, we finally know which components they're ordering. A "live" bill of material is then created for this specific order and that's what gets built. It might look like this:

Customer Order #:	13579
Product Type:	Small Consumer Widget
Quantity:	10
Components:	Control module: CM3
	Sensor: S1
	Power supply: PS3
	Packaging PK14

Note that there is no top-level part number here[7]. That function is served by the customer order number. It goes into the computer with a quantity of 10 in this example, and the components are linked to it via bill of material type records.

Simultaneously, the MPS quantities in the planning bills are reduced accordingly, to avoid duplicating demand. What has happened, therefore, is that uncertainty (in the form of the planning bill) has been replaced by the certainty of the customer order.

You may be wondering about the incoming order rate, given that it might not be level from day to day. Successful users of this planning bill technique frequently will designate one or several very high-volume SKUs as the buffer. When incoming orders are low, they'll make buffer product and put it into inventory (probably using a part number, not an order number). Then, on days when orders are high, they can make all non-buffer products and draw down the buffer inventory on the high volume product(s).

Supporting Make-to-Order

Master Scheduling in pure make-to-order environments is conceptually simpler than in finish-to-order. Make-to-order, as we discussed in Chapter 2, means the company starts to build the product only after the customer order is received[8] — although in some situations, commonly used components are purchased or built in advance of the customer order.

---

7 Although there could be. Some companies do use fixed part numbers; probably more companies do it as shown here.

8 This is conceptually correct, but not always the case in practice. In times of soft demand, when the incoming order volume is low, some make-to-order manufacturers will start jobs into production without a customer order and then adjust priorities as customer orders develop.

We used the example of an aircraft manufacturer, where the basic design of the plane is set ("You can't order a Boeing 757 with four engines.") but customers have a good deal of latitude in specifying things like seating configuration, the placement of galleys and lavatories, and so forth.

Differences between make-to-order and finish-to-order include:

- The role of planning bills in make-to-order is non-existent, or at least much diminished.

- Master Scheduling at more than one level may be done in make-to-order, but there is less interrelationship between the planning entities, such as the common parts bill, modules, and the overall parent product family, as we saw with Small Consumer Widgets.

- In make-to-order, the lower level items are typically *buildable* units. In finish-to order, the common parts bill is usually not a buildable entity, nor are other modules where the common parts have been pulled out and reallocated.

- The use of hedges is diminished in make-to-order.

- Customer order promising tends to be simpler in make-to-order.

Similarities between make-to-order and finish-to-order are:

- The backlog curve applies.

- The Demand Time Fence plays an important role.

- The Master Schedule displays look quite similar.

Most Master Schedulers, if they understand how finish-to-order operates, will have no trouble mastering make-to-order Master Scheduling.

Supporting Design-to-Order

In make-to-order environments, as we just saw, production begins following receipt of the customer order. Most of the product design — but not all of the details — are pretty well set ahead of time. In design-to-order (engineer-to-order), there's less certainty. Although some basic product design has probably been done in order to quote price and delivery, the *detailed product design* begins only after receipt of the customer order.

Production doesn't start until a good bit of the product design is completed. Products made in the design-to-order mode include complex, very specialized machinery. Each one is a new product; the same product is normally never made twice. Being in the design-to-order business has been described as "the selling of a function to the customer for which hardware is designed to accomplish that function."[9]

Here's an example of the difference between design-to-order products and others: A Boeing 767 is a make-to-order product; the Lunar Excursion Module that took Neil Armstrong and his colleagues to the Moon is design-to-order. A Dell personal computer is finish-to-order; the supercomputer resulting from NASA's Beowulf project would be design-to-order.

Some of you may be thinking right about now: "I'm gonna skip this part. This stuff sure doesn't apply to us." Well, before you pull the plug prematurely, hold on for just a moment. The chances are very high that some portion of your business is design-to-order: It's called "new products." Developing and producing new products involve the same kinds of front-end activities that design-to-order companies go through with every product.

From a Master Scheduling standpoint, design-to-order processes are similar to those of make-to-order. The biggest difference is that design-to-order requires a significant amount of up-front project management and scheduling — before the traditional Master Scheduling activities begin.

See Figure 9-8, which shows that early in the creation of the (new) product, project management and scheduling activities and tools such as PERT, Critical Path, and so forth are used exclusively. As more of the details of the product become known, Master Schedule activities begin to kick in. They are used exclusively once the product moves out of the design phase and into production.

Figure 9-8 THE TRANSITION FROM PROJECT SCHEDULING TO MASTER SCHEDULING

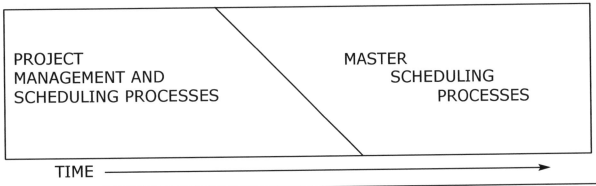

9 William L. Berry, Thomas E. Vollmann, D. Clay Whybark, *Master Production Scheduling: Principles and Practices,* Alexandria, Virginia: APICS, (1984).

Lead times in design-to-order tend to be long. To reduce them a bit, some companies will hedge on long-lead-time materials, either stocking these materials or perhaps ordering them early in the design cycle when there is high probability (although perhaps not 100 percent certainty) that they'll be used in the product being designed.

Capacity Only Master Scheduling

In most companies, a shortage of either materials and/or capacity can mean that production can't happen. In many cases, material availability is more important. For example, materials and components may have long lead times, while additional capacity may be easy to get via the methods we saw earlier.

In other companies, the reverse is true: The overriding issue is capacity — the availability of production time. The materials are rarely a problem.

Mini Case: A Producer of Plastic Film. Company Y supplies highly engineered plastic film and sheeting to a wide variety of consumer products manufacturers, for example disposable diapers. Company Y has very few raw materials, perhaps only several dozen, and keeping them available is hardly ever a problem. Company Y's issue is capacity.

They have a number of extrusion machines, which they call "lines." The key to order promising is matching the customer's request with open time on one of the lines that can produce this product. Some customers require that they certify lines and the products that run on them.

Let's step inside their Customer Order Department. One of the Customer Service Reps, Lynda, is talking to a customer who wants 20,000 pounds of Product #135 in Week 3. The customer service rep knows (or can check easily) that Product #135 is certified to run on line A6 and that a secondary certified line is N7.

Lynda checks the Available-to-Promise for line A6. (See Figure 9-9.) Note that the ATP is by line, not by product. She learns that line A6 is completely sold out for Week 3 but, upon checking line N7, she sees that it can handle 20,000 pounds in Week 3. She so advises the customer and books the order.

Company Y's ability to promise customer orders validly is much better than just a few years ago. So is their order fill rate — up from the low 80 percent range to the high 90s.

Figure 9-9

Capacity Available-to-Promise
(000 pounds)

Line: A6

Week:	1	2	3	4	5	6
Scheduled Capacity:	33	33	33	33	33	33
Customer Orders:	33	33	33	26	18	5
Available-to-Promise : Period				7	15	28
: Cumulative				7	22	50

Line: N7

Week:	1	2	3	4	5	6
Scheduled Capacity:	21	21	21	21	21	21
Customer Orders:	21	15	4			
Available-to-Promise : Period		6	15	21	21	21
: Cumulative		6	21	42	63	84

For businesses like Company Y and others, Master Scheduling capacity rather than products — and then promising customer orders on that basis — can be a very effective way to go.

Coming up in Chapter 10: What do Master Schedulers do, and how do they do it?

Chapter 10

THE MASTER SCHEDULER'S JOB

What makes a good Master Scheduler? Vern Owens, the VP of Operations at the Continental Chemical Company, was facing that very question. He had promoted the current Master Scheduler, Mary Sizemore, to the plant manager's job at their Texas operation. Vern saw the opening created by Mary's departure as an opportunity to review what the Master Scheduler's job is all about.

Vern the VP and Mary the former Master Scheduler met in Conference Room C. They were joined by Connie Stephenson, the Customer Service Manager and Dan Myers, Director of Manufacturing, both of whom had worked very closely with Mary over the past four years. Sheila Conway, the Supply Chain Manager and Mary's direct boss, joined the meeting a bit later.

Vern started the session by saying: "I'd like to brainstorm a bit about this job of Master Scheduling. Specifically, I'd like us to answer these questions:

- What are the characteristics — the traits — of a good Master Scheduler?

- What should the Master Scheduler do? What tasks are involved?

- What tools and other support does the Master Scheduler need to do a first-rate job?"

On the chalkboard that ringed the room, Vern wrote three words, each on a different panel:

<u>Traits</u>　　　　　<u>Tasks</u>　　　　　<u>Tools</u>

They tackled traits first.

Traits (Characteristics) Needed by the Master Scheduler

Mary started off by saying that the Master Scheduler should be faster than a speeding bullet, more powerful than a locomotive, able to leap tall buildings in a single bound, and wear a cape and a sweatshirt with a red S on it. Then they got a bit more serious, and came up with the following traits. Vern made notes on the chalkboard.

Good Product and Customer Knowledge

The Master Scheduler sits at the intersection of demand and supply. On the demand side, a working knowledge about the product and how customers use it can be a big plus, enabling the Master

Scheduler to better understand the issues and the problems faced by customers. This is particularly important when the Master Scheduler has direct contact with customers.

Experience in direct sales, sales support, or marketing, while not a must, can be very helpful, enabling the Master Scheduler to see things through the eyes of the customer.

Good Process Knowledge

Knowing the manufacturing processes used in the plants makes for a more effective Master Scheduler. In many companies, much of the Master Scheduler's job is to develop "Plan B" — also called coping with change. When things go wrong on the plant floor, or a supplier can't deliver, or when customers change their minds, a new plan must be developed and *that plan must be doable*. Good process knowledge makes this much easier. For this reason, experience in the plant or Purchasing (or both) is very desirable.

Good Communication Skills

A failure to communicate is something the Master Scheduler should never be guilty of. Much of the Master Scheduler's job is to facilitate communications between others. This person receives demand information (forecasts, orders, customer schedules, etc.) and translates it into schedules by which the plants and suppliers can meet the customers' needs. When things go wrong and the schedules need to be changed, another round of communications — to both demand and supply people — is often necessary.

In addition, direct communications with top management can be necessary when these decisions involve exceptions to existing strategy or policy, or take on high risk. Wallflowers need not apply.

Good Conflict Resolution Skills

When conflict occurs, the Master Scheduler is expected to bring about resolution. The position itself does not hold decision-making authority, but the Master Scheduler needs to bring others from the demand and supply sides of the business together to make clear decisions. Handling normal and expected conflict between the demand and supply folks is simply part of the job. The Master Scheduler needs to present both sides of a situation, identifying alternative solutions and consequences which others can use to make decisions.

If this person is averse to conflict, problems may get ignored until they fester and finally explode. An effective Master Scheduler will address conflicts early, so that they can be resolved sooner and easier rather than wait until later when resolution will be more difficult. All of this needs to be done in a very dispassionate fashion, which leads to our next characteristic.

Steady, Even Personality

The day-to-day pressure of doing the Master Scheduling job can be substantial. It's impossible to satisfy all of the people all of the time. This job is not for someone who can't handle stress well. A good Master Scheduler should be able to bring a calming influence to what are potentially volatile situations.

Honesty and Integrity

The Master Scheduler deals with many difficult issues in tough circumstances. Honesty, candor, fairness, being upfront, having no hidden agendas — these are all important traits for Master Schedulers. They must earn and maintain the trust and respect of the people with whom they work, both inside and outside the company.

Computer Literacy and Software Knowledge

It's hard to imagine in this day and age, but there may still be a few people out there who can't deal with computers. Those folks will have a hard time in the Master Scheduler's job.

The Master Scheduler should have substantial knowledge of the Master Scheduling software and the larger Enterprise System (ES) of which it's a part. The good news is that the important parts of these software packages can usually be learned in a fairly short time. We'll touch on this software issue again later in this chapter.

Good Administrative Skills

Last but not least, the Master Scheduling job requires the handling of large amounts of information. For this reason, the person should be organized and self-disciplined. Handling the detail, but not getting lost in it, is essential to success.

Back to Conference Room C. Vern's list on the chalkboard looked like this:

TRAITS
Good Product & Customer Knowledge
Good Process Knowledge
Good Communication Skills
Good Conflict Resolution Skills
Steady, Even Personality
Honesty and Integrity
Computer Literacy and Software Knowledge
Good Administrative Skills

Connie asked: "Are these in order of importance? Are the first ones more important than the others?" The consensus was no, and that being honest, trustworthy, and so forth was probably the most important. But by itself, it was not sufficient. Mother Teresa might not have made a very good Master Scheduler; the other traits are essential as well.

As Vern Owens considered this list of characteristics, he wasn't surprised that Mary had done such a fine job as Master Scheduler, gaining his confidence and earning the promotion to plant manager. She had all the personal characteristics: good person, good communicator, good conflict resolver. Further, she had a varied set of prior experiences, starting in the lab as a quality engineer, followed by a tour on the plant floor as a production supervisor. During this time, Mary took and passed the APICS certification exams for production and inventory management. She then became part of the sales support function, working with product application problems in the field, and then moved into Master Scheduling.

Vern also began to realize that the right candidate should be someone from inside the company. This was because learning how to Master Schedule effectively was a big enough job in itself, without adding to it the development of relationships, confidence, and trust. One other thought occurred to Vern — if he found the right person, they too would probably become upwardly mobile, as did Mary. The Master Scheduler's job is a fine training ground for even bigger jobs down the road.

Next, the group turned its attention to the tasks involved in Master Scheduling.

Tasks: What the Master Scheduler Does

Mary started the ball rolling on this topic: "Rather than reinvent the wheel, how about if we look at the job description? I think it's a good one and it certainly seems to be complete." For Consolidated Chemical's Master Scheduler job description, see Figure 10-1.

The group noted that the Master Scheduling job has little or no direct authority, but has a lot of influence about what happens. People in Sales & Marketing and Operations make most of the decisions, and sometimes executive management gets involved. The job of the Master Scheduler is to do the homework necessary to allow these people to see and understand the alternatives and the consequences of their decisions.

Vern smiled and said, "Remember back about two years ago, when that big order from GFE came from out of nowhere? The Sales guys had been trying to crack that account for years with no luck. Our response to that order, both internally and to the customer, was super. That's when I became really confident in our Master Scheduling processes and in Mary's abilities."

Mini Case: A Chemical Manufacturer. Continental Chemical, a fictitious but typical company, is in a very capital-intensive business. The initial cost of chemical reactors is enormous and their designs, until recently, were based on the need for 'economy of scale' and volume. As a result, changeovers are very time-consuming and inefficient. Continental tries to load the equipment to a high percentage of utilization and they change over infrequently to minimize both downtime and off-grade material.

One day, out of the blue, Connie Stephenson in Customer Service received an inquiry for a large order from GFE, a customer that the competition had all locked up . . . until then. Recently the competition was not doing a good job for GFE — almost always shipping late and incomplete.

GFE's inquiry with Continental was to see if they could meet an emergency order. This order was for a large volume of product, required inside of the Planning Time Fence, but if successful, it might mean a substantial amount of additional ongoing business.

Connie contacted Mary, the Master Scheduler, who in turn communicated with Dan, the Manufacturing Director, and with the manager of the Kentucky plant, where most of the product

Figure 10-1

Consolidated Chemical Company
Job Description — Master Scheduler

Basic Function

Convert demands (forecasts, customer orders, customer schedules, etc.) into schedules to assure that matched sets of materials and capacities are available to meet the needs of customers in a cost-effective fashion within the volumes as specified by *Executive S&OP*.

Duties and Responsibilities

1. Contribute to the *Executive S&OP* process, particularly the Supply Planning Step.
2. Participate in the creation of an effective and appropriate Master Scheduling policy.
3. Load the Master Schedule through the Planning Time Fence to the volume specified by the Production Plan from the Executive S&OP process.
4. Identify, negotiate, and bring to resolution any demand/supply imbalances in both volume and mix.
5. Review and manage change requests from customers, plants, and suppliers, making appropriate reschedules in accordance with the Master Schedule policy.
6. Recognize the need to maintain stability in the Master Schedule, while being responsive to the needs of customers.
7. Allow no past due's in the Master Schedule.
8. Develop and maintain planning data, such as: Planning Bills of Material, Safety Stock, Lead Times, Lot Sizes, etc.
9. Monitor forecast consumption and the proper use of Available-to-Promise.
10. Inform the appropriate individuals, per the Master Schedule policy, of any issues that cannot be handled within the framework of that policy.

Method of Measurement

- Managing the Master Schedule to stay within +/- 2 percent of the Production Plan as authorized in Executive S&OP.
- Enabling the plant to achieve 95 percent or greater performance of the Master Schedule for dates and quantities within specified tolerances.
- Holding action messages at 10 percent or less of items being Master Scheduled.
- Maintaining zero past due within the Master Schedule.

Reporting Relationship

The Master Scheduler reports to the Supply Chain Manager.

in question was made. Mary asked them a lot of questions prior to getting down to the nitty gritty: to figure out what could be done to accept this order and to determine the consequences of doing so.

The outcome of the Master Scheduler's research resulted in the following alternatives:

1. Accept the order and reschedule one of the current customers already promised. This would mean going back on a promise to a current customer. This alternative would also increase cost because it would involve an additional changeover.

2. Purchase product from a source outside the company, resulting in a very small profit and perhaps a loss. Also, they weren't too sure about the source's quality.

3. Produce the product at the Utah plant and ship it to GFE's location in North Carolina at considerable additional expense, resulting in a loss on this order.

The VP of Sales & Marketing indicated that the needs of all existing customers had to be met as scheduled. The Plant Manager's position was that he could not take on additional sales volume without incurring significant costs and thus jeopardizing the plant's profit goals for the fiscal year. Thus this situation could quite likely affect the business plan, and carry a significant degree of risk. Mary briefed the vice presidents of Sales/Marketing and of Operations, outlining the alternatives, their opportunities, and the costs involved.

That meeting was reconvened the following morning and enlarged to include the VP of Finance and the President. Once again, Mary detailed the alternatives with their attendant good news/bad news. The group made their decision, accepted the order, produced it in Utah thereby losing a few dollars on freight, shipped it on time and complete, and captured a substantial amount of ongoing volume from their competition. That's when it first occurred to Vern that Master Scheduling had become a significant value-add — and a competitive weapon — to the company.

Even though the Master Scheduler does not normally have line authority, s/he does exercise large amounts of judgment. That judgment is to make things happen within existing policy, strategy, and business conditions. When this can't be done, the Master Scheduler needs to raise the issues and problems with the proper authority for changing the constraints or accepting the consequences.

In some cases, the Master Scheduling job is a full-time position; in others it's part-time depending on:

- The complexity of the products and processes

- The volatility of the customers and marketplace

- Centralized (at the general office) or decentralized (at the plants)

- The volume of items being Master Scheduled

- Supervisory responsibilities

When the job of Master Scheduling is less than a full-time position, it is often combined with responsibilities such as: production control manager, plant scheduler, assistant plant manager, finite scheduler, supplier scheduler, customer order department manager, forecast analyst, and the like.

Although the Master Scheduler may report administratively to either the demand or supply side of the business, they should not see themselves as aligned with either one. To some degree, they must blur the distinctions between departments, balancing responsiveness to stability, plant productivity to inventory, and cost to customer's needs. Thus the Master Scheduling job is *both* demand and supply related.

Back to Conference Room C. The group concluded that the current job description did an adequate job of spelling out the tasks involved in Master Scheduling. Vern wrote on the chalkboard:

TASKS
See job description

Next Vern said, "Let's tackle tools, and then we can go to lunch."

Tools: What the Master Scheduler Needs

A Master Scheduling Policy with Teeth

"Well," said Mary, "the first thing that comes to my mind is the Master Scheduling policy. Without that, I'd have been hung out to dry dozens of times." Before we had that policy, people would duck decisions that only they should make. That would leave the decision pretty much up to me and — in most cases — I wouldn't have nearly as much knowledge and information as they did.

"Of course, the opposite of that happened also: Sometimes they'd unilaterally tell me to make a change to the schedule that should have had buy-in from another part of the business. This happened a lot with abnormal demand. Let me tell you, it's pretty difficult to say 'no' to someone with a VP title who's two levels above you in the organization. Right, Vern?

"Anyhow, after we created the Master Scheduling policy, that all went away. I can't imagine anyone being able to do a first-rate job of Master Scheduling without a policy statement like this."

The Master Scheduling policy is a concise but complete document that details roles and responsibilities. Authorized and signed by top management, it spells out to the Master Scheduler and others on both the demand and supply sides of the business, who owes what to whom. It specifies who is empowered to make decisions and under what circumstances. See Figure 10-2 for a sample Master Scheduling policy.

Accurate Data

Unless a company is completely make-to-order or design-to-order, the Master Scheduler can be crippled by bad inventory records. In a make-to-stock situation, the on-hand inventory balances of the finished products must be highly accurate. In finish-to-order environments, high accuracy is required on the inventory balances of completed modules, intermediates, and other components waiting to be used on the final products.

In a broader sense, high accuracy is required on many other items necessary to make the overall resource planning processes (ERP) work well: bills of material, routings, and so forth.[1] These items can *indirectly* impact the Master Scheduler, because they can prevent the proper functioning of material planning, supplier scheduling, and plant scheduling, thus preventing the Master Schedule from being properly executed. We're stressing inventory accuracy here because it *directly* affects the Master Scheduler's ability to do his or her job. More on this in Chapter 11.

Good Software

It's possible to do Master Scheduling manually. This is particularly true in Lean Manufacturing environments, where we've seen some creative approaches to manual Master Scheduling (some good and some not so good). However, most companies — Lean or otherwise — use some degree of computer support for Master Scheduling; they feel it's simply too time consuming and error prone to do manually.

---

[1] For more on data integrity requirements in an ERP environment, see Wallace and Kremzar, *ERP: Making It Happen*, New York: John Wiley & Sons (2001).

Figure 10-2

Sample Master Scheduling Policy

Objective: The Master Schedule balances demand and supply at the mix level. It extends sufficiently into the future to cover the lead times associated with detailed material and capacity planning, and is defined by the Planning Time Fence. Both Sales/Marketing and Operations play a significant part in its proper management. The Master Scheduler's role is to facilitate and monitor adherence to policy in this regard.

Specific Issues:

- The Master Schedule summed by family must equal (within a specified tolerance) the Production Plan as specified by the Executive S&OP process (or its equivalent).

- The Master Schedule must be achievable, assuring specific material and capacity availability.

- Decision-making authority to change the Master Schedule within the Planning Time Fence does not rest solely with the Master Scheduler. The attachment to this document defines who can authorize changes within the PTF, and this varies by type of product, the magnitude of the change, and when the change is desired.

- In the event that agreement cannot be reached regarding a requested change, the General Manager will make the decision.

- Sales and Customer Order Entry must use Available-to-Promise in making customer commitments.

- Forecasts are maintained by Sales/Marketing and are properly consumed by customer orders.

- Exception messages are monitored and acted upon, and the principle of "no past due" is adhered to.

- On-time plant performance to the Master Production Schedule is 95 percent or higher and the plant is held accountable.

- Stability within the Master Schedule is essential, and changes to the Master Schedule are measured and managed to an acceptable level. Within the Planning Time Fence, the number of MPSs rescheduled in should approximately equal the number rescheduled out.

- The Master Scheduler chairs the weekly meeting between Sales/Marketing and Operations to review issues, performance, and problems related to shipments and production.

To be effective, Master Scheduling software must:

- be reasonably complete in terms of functionality: forecast consumption, Available-to-Promise, projected available balance, time fences, and so forth.

- be based on standard logic[2]. If the software won't consume the forecast properly, for example, the Master Scheduler will have a very difficult time being successful.

- be easy to understand and easy to use. Complexity is bad; simplicity is good.

Support

Last but not least is the issue of support. The Master Scheduler, as we've said more than once, is the guy or gal "in the middle." It's a tough job. Guided by the Master Scheduling policy, s/he'll sometimes have to say "no." Once again, you can't please all of the people all of the time.

What can help is an awareness by the Master Scheduler's primary internal customers — Sales & Marketing, Operations, General Management — that it is a tough job. These people should let that awareness guide their relationships with the Master Scheduler. Praise is appreciated. A well-placed "good job" or "thank you" can make a difference.

Vern finished adding these points to the chalkboard:

TOOLS
Master Scheduling Policy with Teeth
Accurate Data
Good Software
Support

The group looked at these for a bit, and then checked the other two panels:

---

2 An excellent reference work here is Darryl Landvater and Chris Gray's book: *MRPII: The Standard System*, New York: John Wiley & Sons (1989).

TRAITS	TASKS
Good Product & Customer Knowledge	See job description
Good Process Knowledge	
Good Communication Skills	
Good Conflict Resolution Skills	
Steady, Even Personality	
Honesty and Integrity	
Computer Literacy and Software Knowledge	
Good Administrative Skills	

They liked what they saw. There were smiles and nodding heads. No one came up with anything to add, and it was time for lunch.

Chapter 11

MAKING MASTER SCHEDULING WORK

How do you know if your Master Scheduling processes aren't working well? If you're experiencing one or more of the following, it's time to make some changes.

- **Unreliable promises and missed customer deliveries.** This means you can't do what you say you're going to do and thus you are routinely disappointing your customers.

- **The "end-of-the-month lump."** Also called the hockey stick effect, it refers to shipping about 80 percent of the month's volume in the last 20 percent of the month in order to hit the month's shipping budget. It's expensive, bad for quality, and routinely disappoints the customers.

- **Substantial expediting.** When the formal planning and scheduling tools don't work, the informal system takes over. The informal system isn't written up in the policy and procedures manual. Rather it exists in hot lists, red tags, out sheets, and the like.

- **Time inefficiency.** It takes frequent meetings with lots of people to be able to get product out the door.

- **Finger pointing.** To people caught in the middle of the informal system, it invariably seems that "it's the other guy's fault." There's no valid game plan to which people can be held accountable. Thus the salespeople blame Production; production people blame Purchasing; the purchasing people blame Scheduling; the scheduling people blame Sales and on and on.

- **Simultaneous shortages and excess inventory.** Again, thanks to the informal system: lots of inventory, but the wrong stuff.

The above set of conditions is counterproductive and time consuming. These problems drain energy that could be better used elsewhere, and they are not fun. There has to be a better way — and there is.

Starting Over

Most companies today are doing some form of Master Scheduling; few are starting from scratch. In most cases, making Master Scheduling work is a matter of fixing what's wrong rather than starting with a brand new implementation. However, the jobs involved in fixing a broken Master Scheduling process are much the same as implementing Master Scheduling for the first time. We'll focus first on reimplementation — starting over — and then later in this chapter we'll double back and focus on first-time implementers.

Better tools for decision making — and Master Scheduling is certainly one of these — normally involve three major elements: the computer software (and hardware of course), the data, and the people who use the tool. Implementing these tools involves each one of these elements and *each one of them has to be done right*. Two out of three is not good enough.

It's important to know that all three of these elements are essential, but that's still not enough. Some of these items are more important — far more important — than others. Therefore, only when a company knows which items are more or less important can the company prioritize its efforts and apply its limited resources effectively.

Well, what's a good tool to help prioritize? If you answered Pareto, you're absolutely correct. The Pareto approach, one of the more widely used tools in the Total Quality toolkit, is derived from Pareto's Law, which concerns the vital few and the less important many. As we said in our book on Sales Forecasting, this is often seen in inventory management: The relatively few A items are the ones with high impact, dollars or otherwise, while the many C items have low impact. The B items are the ones in the middle. An important point about the C items: They can be essential, frequently needed to make a shipment. So the issue is not one of necessity, but one of impact and importance. The C items are essential, but of less significance. The company should devote less time to the C items than the As.

The ABC, Pareto-based approach also applies to decision-making processes such as Master Scheduling and resource planning processes:

The C item is the computer software and hardware.
Essential, but not the critically important item.

The B item is the data.
The validity and utility of the input data is of
more significance than the computer.

The A item is the people.
The success of any initiative to improve decision-making
processes will depend almost totally on the people:
their dedication, their willingness, their knowledge.

The C-item — Software

Now, given all that, our next point shouldn't come as a big surprise: In virtually all dysfunctional Master Scheduling processes, the problem is *not* in the software. Replacing or "fixing" the Master Scheduling software is usually not the place to start, even though the software may lack some of the features one might hope for. If you focus heavily on the software, the C item, you'll be working at the margins thereby neglecting the truly important elements — and you will probably not be successful.

In the unlikely event that your Master Scheduling software is so bad that it simply can't be made to work, we recommend that you not automatically decide to get an entire new suite of Enterprise-wide Software (ES). This will take a long time: search, selection, modification, and installation across almost all of the functions in the company. You probably can't do all that in less than a year, which means you're faced with many more months of the bad stuff we've talked about for the last ten chapters: missed shipments, high inventories, finger pointing, and so on.

Rather, consider buying an inexpensive, simple, stand-alone Master Scheduling package that you can bridge to your current systems and use successfully. Then, should you decide later to go with an Enterprise-wide Software suite, you can convert over to the Master Scheduling module in the ES and drop the stand-alone software.

Keep the C-item the C-item. Don't let the software tail wag the total company dog.

The B-item — Data

Master Scheduling uses a lot of data; some of it needs to be highly accurate and others less so. Some data impacts Master Scheduling directly and can keep it from working properly. Also, bad data in other parts of the ERP processes — for example MRP, Plant Scheduling, Supplier Scheduling — can inhibit those elements from working. This, of course, can impact unfavorably on the Master Schedule by preventing it from being executed.

It's also important to distinguish between *forgiving* and *unforgiving* data. Forgiving data includes things like lead times, lot sizes, safety stocks, standards, and the like; it does not require high accuracy. As long as the numbers are reasonable and pretty much "in the ballpark," you'll be fine. Therefore, you don't need to spend enormous amounts of time on getting these numbers super-accurate; they're not the priority.

Unforgiving data, on the other hand, will kill Master Scheduling quickly and without mercy. These are the numbers that need to be very, very accurate: inventory records, bills of material, and routings. Also in this unforgiving category are open order status for production and purchasing: correct due dates, quantities, and the identification of the supplier, work center, and so forth.

So, to take a look at how this unforgiving data impacts Master Scheduling both directly and indirectly, see Figure 11-1.

Figure 11-1

UNFORGIVING DATA AND ITS IMPACT ON THE MASTER SCHEDULE

Type of Master Scheduling Process	Affects Master Scheduling Directly	Affects Master Scheduling Indirectly (through MRP, Plant Scheduling, Supplier Scheduling, etc.)
Make-to-stock	Finished Goods Inventory Records	Component and Material Inventory Records
		Bills of Material
	Bills of Material Routings	Routings
Finish-to-order	Module Inventory Records	Component and Material Inventory Records
	Planning Bills of Material	Standard Bills of Material
		Routings
Make-to-order		Component and Material Inventory Records
		Bills of Material
		Routings
Design-to-order		Component and Material Inventory Records
		Bills of Material
		Routings

Unforgiving Data — Inventory Records

People in make-to-stock and finish-to-order businesses should be aware that effective Master Scheduling requires highly accurate inventory balances for finished goods and completed modules. Think about it — what results when the inventory balances are wrong?

- Invalid customer order promising because the Available-to-Promise information is wrong.

- Bad projected inventory balances and open order status, which cause erroneous action messages.

- Master Production Schedules (MPSs) that are incorrect in timing or quantity, or possibly both.

The end result: People don't use the Master Schedule as part of doing their job because they can't trust it. It always gets them in trouble. So they revert back to the informal system because, even with all its problems, they know how to use it to get product shipped.

How accurate do your inventory records need to be? At least 95 percent — and that refers not to dollars but to units. Ninety five percent, minimum, of all the inventory records in the computer must match what's in the real world. If you don't have this, it's unlikely that you'll ever have a first-rate Master Scheduling process.[1]

Some people maintain that with Lean Manufacturing, accurate inventory records aren't needed. That's partially true. From an execution perspective, Lean is highly visual; "If the pallet is empty, then the inventory is zero regardless of what the computer thinks it is." However, when the inventory records are used in medium- to long-range planning, they must be accurate or invalid information will be generated and the planning process will be out of sync with the execution side. The additional good news with Lean is that there's not much inventory in the first place, so getting the records accurate is much easier.

Unforgiving Data — Bills of Material and Routings

For make-to-stock products, bill of material errors directly affect the Master Schedule. Further, if you're operating a two-level Master Scheduling process, you're almost certainly using Planning Bills of Material. Thus, these *directly* affect the validity of the Master Schedule. For example, if a given product can take Options A, B, C, or D — and the planning bill calls out Options A, B, C, or F — that is an incorrect planning bill.

---

1 Roger Brooks and Larry Wilson have written a fine book on this topic: *Inventory Record Accuracy,* New York: John Wiley & Sons, (1993).

Bill of material errors affect the Master Schedule *indirectly* for subassemblies, intermediates, and individual manufactured items. These kinds of errors can lead to shortages and thus the inability to execute the Master Schedule.

We recommend a minimum of 98 percent accuracy on bills of material. This means that 98 percent of all *single-level* bills of material should be correct as to component identification, quantity per, and unit of measure. (For more on this topic, please see *Manufacturing Data Structures* by Jerry Clement, Andy Coldrick, John Sari. Essex Junction, VT: Oliver Wight Limited Publications, [1992] p. 61–72.)

In many companies, routings carry less significance today than they did twenty years ago, and much of that is due to Lean Manufacturing. Complex, job shop forms of manufacturing organization are converted to in-line, linear flow processes; the routings then become more defined by the physical placement of equipment and people rather than by words and numbers on a piece of paper.

Regardless, routings are still used in many companies and errors here can impact the Master Schedule. Minimum accuracy for routings is 98 percent correct as to the operations to be performed, the work centers involved, and the sequence of each operation. Here also, you may want to check the *Manufacturing Data Structures* book.

Note that standards are not included in this list. That's because they're forgiving; they don't need to be highly accurate in order to enable effective capacity planning and plant scheduling.

The A-item — People

For the people — the most important element in a successful Master Scheduling endeavor — to be effective, two things must happen. First, they should know what to do and why. Second, they should be skilled in managing the process to achieve its goals. The first part of the equation comes about via education and training.

Education and Training

These two words are not synonymous. They actually refer to quite different things:

1. Education for Master Scheduling means learning what it is, why it's necessary, how to use it effectively in different environments, and so forth. Education gets at *how to run the business* with this superior tool called Master Scheduling — and how that relates to Executive S&OP and the other Resource Planning elements.

2. Training is largely computer-focused. It talks about things like the details of screen formats, what keys to hit to release a Master Production Schedule, how to change the Planning Time Fence, and so forth. Training centers on *how to run the software.*

Many companies make the mistake of training but not educating. You need to do both. You can't just teach people the details of what to do, but not the big picture of why and how and what's involved.

Actually, more people in the company will need education on Master Scheduling than training. Why? Because relatively few people will be operating the Master Scheduling software[2], but the actions of many people can affect the Master Schedule: Sales & Marketing, Purchasing, Plant Floor, and — oh yes — top management. Most of these folks won't require a lot of education, but they do need to know the what's, why's, and high-level how's of Master Scheduling.

Why top management? Think about it: How will they be able to intelligently question, modify, and authorize the Master Scheduling policy if they don't understand what Master Scheduling is all about? And down the road, how will they avoid making uninformed, potentially damaging decisions if they haven't been informed as to how this process works.

An example of an uninformed decision: the General Manager saying, "Book that new order and put it early in the Master Schedule. That'll motivate the troops. Don't bother me about overloads." The result of this decision is to overload the Master Schedule, which invalidates its priorities, which ruins its credibility, which means the informal system (which is always lurking in the wings) will come back and take over — along with all of the problems that go with it.

Top management doesn't need the nitty-gritty details of Master Scheduling, but they do need to *understand* what makes it work and what makes it fail.

Training materials are easy to get; they come with the software. Education materials are more varied. They include this book and others, video courses, and courses given by APICS and other reputable organizations. For details see Appendix B, Bibliography.

Managing the Master Scheduling Process

We can start this section very simply: If you don't have a written, authorized Master Scheduling policy, get started on one now and finish it within a month or so. Remember, you'll need to educate some people before you can get widespread participation in developing this policy. You may

---

2 However, these folks, the primary users, will need a great deal of training in addition to the education they must receive.

want to revisit your order fulfillment strategies — make-to-stock, finish-to-order, and so forth — for changes that either have occurred, or should occur, because these kinds of changes can impact the Master Scheduling environment.

Once the policy is authorized and in place, run the business by what it says. A note to current and future Master Schedulers: As we saw in the last chapter, a Master Scheduling Policy — authorized by top management — is essential; don't leave home without it.

Next, for those of you already doing Master Scheduling, we need to talk about a task that almost all of you will face: fixing an overloaded Master Schedule. Most dysfunctional Master Schedules have a bunch of Master Production Schedules in the past due time period plus a lot more in the first several weeks. This volume of work is typically not producible in the time periods specified; it far exceeds the plant's capacity (as shown in Figure 11-2).

In Figure 11-2, each of the MPSs making up this workload has a work content of 20 hours. (That's to keep the example simple and easy to follow.)

Okay, so this line is horribly overloaded. It has more work than it can accomplish for the first five weeks; only in Week 6 does it "catch up" (another example of ten pounds of potatoes in a five-pound bag). Further, let's assume that Line 2 is the only line capable of making these products. We can get no help from sister plants, nor from contract manufacturers.

What should be done? If you're content with business as usual, do nothing. Live with a bad situation and do the best you can with the informal system. However, if you want to make Master Scheduling work and reap the sizeable benefits, then you will need to take action.

The load will have to be leveled out. This means moving MPSs in the early weeks to later weeks, thereby shifting the early overload to later periods where there's more room. In Figure 11-3 we can see the results of doing that: The load has been shifted to the right and thereby has been leveled.

Looks easy, right? It's just a matter of rescheduling some Master Production Schedules: three out of Week 1 and the Past Due, two from Week 2, and one from Week 3. Then, don't put any new MPSs into the schedule unless there's capacity available to do so. It's that simple, right?

Wrong. Here's another case where the mechanics are easy, but getting agreement to do it is not. Those MPSs to be rescheduled out probably have customer orders tied to them. So then the question arises: Which customer orders will we re-promise: The Jones order? The Smith order? The Acme order? The Continental order?

Figure 11-2

AN OVERLOADED ROUGH-CUT CAPACITY PLAN

LINE 2 — in Standard Hours

	Week 1 + PAST DUE	Week 2	Week 3	Week 4	Week 5	Week 6
WORKLOAD # of MPS hours	8 160	7 140	6 120	4 80	1 20	0 0
DEMONSTRATED CAPACITY (hrs)	100	100	100	100	100	100
DIFFERENCE	-60	-40	-20	20	80	100
CUMULATIVE DIFF	-60	-100	-120	-100	-20	80

Figure 11-3

A LEVELED ROUGH-CUT CAPACITY PLAN

LINE 2 — in Standard Hours

	Week 1 + PAST DUE	Week 2	Week 3	Week 4	Week 5	Week 6
WORKLOAD # of MPS hours	5 100	5 100	5 100	5 100	5 100	1 20
DEMONSTRATED CAPACITY (hrs)	100	100	100	100	100	100
DIFFERENCE	0	0	0	0	0	80
CUMULATIVE DIFF	0	0	0	0	0	80

Here again, education can make the difference. It can help the Sales people understand what Master Scheduling's about. They'll understand that not all of those orders are going to get shipped, and that they should grab hold of the situation and specify proactively *which* orders will ship in *which* weeks. Then the company can get down to the business of doing what it says it's going to do: ship product to customers on time.

Once last point: Let's say that, despite your best efforts, you still can't get agreement for this rescheduling/unloading process. All may not be lost, provided that people will agree to:

1. Let the overload work itself off over time. In other words, don't put any more MPSs in the overloaded time period. Take another look at Figure 11-2: The first week with open capacity is Week 6, and that's the earliest any new MPSs should be scheduled.

2. Once the necessary time has passed and the overload is gone, do not allow a new overload to be created. Keep the Master Schedule valid, and that means no overloads. This is one more example of why the Master Schedule policy is so important.

Starting from Scratch

First-time implementers of Master Scheduling may have an easier job than the reimplementers: They're starting with a clean slate and probably don't have to go through the hassle of dealing with an overloaded Master Schedule. Besides that, everything we've said in the prior sections on starting over also applies to companies starting from scratch.

Virtually all first-time implementations of Master Scheduling occur within the framework of a larger implementation — that of an entire Enterprise Resource Planning (ERP) initiative. This is where *all* of the Enterprise-wide Software (ES) is installed, *all* of the data is made accurate, and *all* of the people receive education and training.

There's a lot involved in one of these projects, including a fundamental decision as to whether to implement ERP on a unified, company-wide basis or via a "quick slice" approach: one major product group at a time. These issues are far beyond the scope of this book, and we refer to reader to the book mentioned earlier, *ERP: Making It Happen.*

Some companies — more than a few — have purchased Enterprise-wide Software and installed it on their computers, but have not implemented the set of business processes and decision-making tools called ERP. That includes Master Scheduling. Thus they're first-time implementers, but they've got a leg up: They already have the software they'll need to make these processes work. (This assumes that the software suite they purchased is adequate or better, which is normally the case.)

The Master Scheduling Effectiveness Checklist

The ultimate measure of successful Master Scheduling is its contribution to the business goals of higher service, quicker response, lower inventories, reduced costs, enhanced control of the business, and superior financial performance. Obviously, Master Scheduling alone can't bring about all these results. It is, however, an important contributor to these goals and so the ultimate yardstick of the success of Master Scheduling is how many of these improvements the company realizes.

There is another approach to measuring effectiveness: the process audit. This tends to be more specific and focuses on what are called *enabling* measurements. These elements — process steps, data integrity, accountabilities, and the like — are the foundation that enables the achievement of the *resulting* measurements of customer service, speed, inventory turns, and so forth. They're listed in a checklist format in Figure 11-4.

We recommend that reimplementers begin using this checklist right away to help evaluate how well – or poorly – their Master Scheduling processes are working. The approach here is to rate the company's status using 4 (Excellent, we're doing that very well - no further improvement needed), 3 (Good, we're doing that well but we could do better), 2 (Fair, we're doing some of that but need to improve a lot), 1 (Poor, we're not doing that at all and we need to do it very well) or N/A (this does not apply to our business).

The intent here is to improve the Master Scheduling process. This is accomplished by making improvements in the process, thereby convert the 1s to 2s, the 2s to 3s, and the 3s to 4s.

First-time implementers can use this checklist as a kind of roadmap to help them focus on accomplishing what needs to be done in order to achieve a first-rate process. They could begin using the checklist several weeks after they've begun implementation and then review it once every several weeks thereafter until the process is implemented and running properly.

Following a successful implementation or reimplementation, reviewing the checklist once every three to six months should suffice. Readers should feel free to photocopy the checklist; it's an important tool and should be used periodically to help run the business better.

Figure 11-4

The Master Scheduling Effectiveness Checklist

	Ex	Gd	Fr	Pr
1. A written Master Scheduling policy has been established, authorized by top management, and is used to help manage the business. Principle M14: Effectively dealing with change — in both demand and supply — is the essence of successful Master Scheduling.	4	3	2	1
2. The Master Scheduling policy defines accountabilities for decision-making: who is authorized to make decisions in which time zones and under what circumstances. Principle M14: Effectively dealing with change — in both demand and supply — is the essence of successful Master Scheduling.	4	3	2	1
3. The Master Schedule is maintained to achieve the desired balance between stability and responsiveness. It is widely recognized throughout the company that the stability of the Master Schedule is important, and that it leads to manufacturing and supply chain responsiveness. Principle M13: The Master Scheduler must see the true demand. When remote stocking points exist, their demand is dependent upon how those remote points will be replenished.	4	3	2	1
4. The Master Schedule is in weekly or smaller increments.	4	3	2	1
5. Changes to the Master Schedule inside the Planning Time Fence are carefully managed to the availability of specific materials and capacity. Principle M10: The Master Schedule can the basis for customer order promising, via its Available-to-Promise feature.	4	3	2	1
6. Outside the Planning Time Fence, most forecasting and planning is done in the aggregate, using the data from Executive S&OP.	4	3	2	1
7 The Planning Time Fence for products and key components sourced off-shore is set with full recognition of the long lead times normally involved.	4	3	2	1
8. The Master Scheduler is active and engaged in the Executive S&OP process. Principle M1: The Master Schedule must be managed to closely match the Operations Plan authorized by top management in the Executive S&OP process.	4	3	2	1
9. The Master Scheduler is in frequent communication with key personnel from both the demand and supply sides of the business, for purposes of problem anticipation and resolution. Principle M14: Effectively dealing with change — in both demand and supply — is the essence of successful Master Scheduling.	4	3	2	1

	Ex	Gd	Fr	Pr
10. The Master Scheduler is constantly aware of the potential inventory exposure and risk at the contract manufacturers, and proactivley takes steps to eliminate risk.	4	3	2	1

Principle M6: The Master Schedule must be under human control. The computer recommends; people decide.

	Ex	Gd	Fr	Pr
11. Feedback from Purchasing and Production is routinely provided regarding orders that will be late and their repromised dates.	4	3	2	1

Principle M7: The due dates in the Master Schedule must be valid. They must accurately reflect when production orders will be completed and when customer orders will be shipped.

	Ex	Gd	Fr	Pr
12. The company uses Planning Bills of Material, Two-Level Master Scheduling, Hedging, and so on where appropriate, or if not, routinely evaluates their potential.	4	3	2	1

Principles M4 & M5: M4 Where practical, utilize the concept of Postponement: Hold off adding optional features into the product until after the customer order is received. Structure your products, your production processes, and your forecasting and scheduling processes to take advantage of Postponement. M5. Finish-to-order is the best order fulfillment strategy for most companies in most industries. It is more efficient and flexible than make-to-stock, and has shorter lead times than make-to-order.

	Ex	Gd	Fr	Pr
13. The Master Schedule is kept up-to-date; it is maintained to reflect current conditions and no past due data is allowed.	4	3	2	1

Principle M7: The due dates in the Master Schedule must be valid. They must accurately reflect when production orders will be completed and when customer orders will be shipped.

	Ex	Gd	Fr	Pr
14. Effective communications processes are in place between the Master Schedulers and their coutnrparts at contract manufactures.	4	3	2	1

Principle M6: The Master Schedule must be under human control. The computer recommends; people decide.

	Ex	Gd	Fr	Pr
15. The Master Schedule has visibility into all known demands: customer orders, distribution, interplant, samples, and so on.	4	3	2	1

Principle M12: The Master Schedule and the Finishing Schedule are rarely the same thing. The Finishing Schedule is derived from the Master Schedule and is focused on short-term supply.

	Ex	Gd	Fr	Pr
16. In order to reach target customer service levels, safety stocks for products and components sourced off-shore are set higher than for domestically sourced products, to compensate for greater lead time and supply variability.	4	3	2	1

	Ex	Gd	Fr	Pr
17. To the extent possible, Master Scheduling of outsourced products employs the same people and processes as for in-house products.	4	3	2	1

Principle M6: The Master Schedule must be under human control. The computer recommends; people decide.

	Ex	Gd	Fr	Pr
18. Proper forecast consumption techniques are used.	4	3	2	1

Principle M8: Silence is approval. The Master Scheduler has every right to assume that products will be completed as scheduled, unless notified by Production or Purchasing that there will be a delay.

	Ex	Gd	Fr	Pr
19. Customer orders are promised via the Available-to-Promise or Capable-to-Promise technique, where appropriate.	4	3	2	1

Principle M9: Valid forecast consumption is essential for Master Scheduling to work properly.

	Ex	Gd	Fr	Pr
20. The Master Scheduler is notified as soon as possible regarding abnormal demands entering the company.	4	3	2	1

Principle M14: Effectively dealing with change — in both demand and supply — is the essence of successful Master Scheduling.

	Ex	Gd	Fr	Pr
21. Simulation is routinely used to evluate alternative solutions to problems and opportunites.	4	3	2	1

Principle M14: Effectively dealing with change — in both demand and supply — is the essence of successful Master Scheduling.

	Ex	Gd	Fr	Pr
22. Distribution Requirements Planning (DRP) is used where appropriate.	4	3	2	1

Principle M12: The Master Schedule and the Finishing Schedule are rarely the same thing. The Finishing Schedule is derived from the Master Schedule, and is focused on short-term supply.

	Ex	Gd	Fr	Pr
23. The sum of the Master Schedule is maintained to equal the Operations Plan authorized by top management in Executive S&OP.	4	3	2	1

Principle M1: The Master Schedule must be managed to closely match the Operations Plan authorized by top management in the Executive S&OP process.

	Ex	Gd	Fr	Pr
24. The Master Schedule's impact on capacity is continuously monitored; overloaded Master Schedules are not permitted.	4	3	2	1

Principle M10: The Master Schedule can be the basis for customer order promising via its Available-to-Promise feature.

	Ex	Gd	Fr	Pr
25. Capacity constraints at contract manufacturers are known by the persons doing the master scheduling for those items, and they take those constraints into account when setting the schedules.	4	3	2	1

Principle M10: The Master Schedule can be the basis for customer order promising via its Available-to-Promise feature.

	Ex	Gd	Fr	Pr
26. Demonstrated capacity data is updated at least quarterly, reflecting recent activity.	4	3	2	1

Principle M10: The Master Schedule can be the basis for customer order promising via its Available-to-Promise feature.

	Ex	Gd	Fr	Pr
27. The Finishing (Final Assembly) Schedules derived from and maintained in sync with the Master Schedule.	4	3	2	1

Principle M11: You can't put ten pounds in a five pound bag. Effective Capacity Planning processes are necessary to ensure that supply is in balance with demand.

SCORING FOR MASTER SCHEDULING CHECKLIST

# of 4s: _   * 4 = _

# of 3s: _   * 3 = _

# of 2s: _   * 2 = _

# of 1s: _   * 1 = _

TOTAL = _

TOTAL _   divided by: _   (27 minus # of NAs) = SCORE _

Score evaluation: 3.5 - 4.0 = Excellent

3.0 - 3.4 = Good

2.0 - 2.9 = Fair

<2.0   = Poor

Please remember: the purpose here is to make things better. Use this checklist as a guide for improvement.

One last point: When Master Scheduling is working well, you should be able to *feel* it. It feels like the people are running the plant, not vice versa. And that feeling comes about through the people's ability to manage changes as they arise, and not to allow the changes to disrupt the operation. Here's an important principle of Master Scheduling:

Principle #14: Effectively dealing with change — in both demand and supply — is the essence of successful Master Scheduling.

Epilogue

A LOOK FORWARD

At the beginning of the 20th century, most of America's population was involved in agriculture, living and working on family farms. It took that many people to feed themselves and the rest of the U.S. population.

During the last century, an amazing transformation occurred in agriculture. Far greater knowledge of the dynamics of growing plants, the adoption of advanced chemical processes for fertilization, the widespread use of automation through machinery, and other factors have enabled farmers to generate yields and efficiencies that were undreamed of in the year 1900. Today most people are aware that the reason for starvation in the world is not production but rather distribution. The food exists, but sometimes it can't be moved to the point of need.

Today, early in the 21st century, only a few Americans are engaged in farming, but they can produce an enormous amount. It's alleged that American farmers, if left to their own abilities and resources, could feed *the entire world*. What an amazing transformation!

Something similar is happening in manufacturing. We are able to produce more products today with fewer people. This trend has been present for some time and it will continue. Will we ever get to the same pinnacle of output and efficiency as agriculture? Will a fraction of the population be able to produce all goods needed by the entire world? We doubt it, but we do know that we're heading in that general direction.

That's why, when your authors see economic reports citing that manufacturing employment is flat or dropping, we don't always view it as bad news. Yes, we feel sorry for the people who are out of work and yes, we are concerned about job loss to offshore. Regarding this latter point, it seems to us that all of the jobs that have gone offshore can be divided into two categories:

1. Jobs with high labor content that will stay offshore for the foreseeable future, due to the much lower wage rates in some parts of the world. (And that's not all bad news when one considers the impact of wages on our standard of living.)

2. Jobs that went offshore but should be brought back because:

   a. the labor component of the product cost isn't all that large and thus the total supply chain costs such as freight, inventories, and the like are equal to or greater than if the product were made domestically.

   b. the marketplace is demanding more and more product variety and quicker and quicker response. This can be hard to do from half a world away.

As American manufacturing becomes increasingly proficient at using the tools in the toolkit (see the list below), and as customers continue to raise the bar higher for speed and variety, we can expect more jobs to be brought back from offshore. But that won't change the overall trend.

Flat or declining employment in manufacturing is a normal process and we expect it to continue for the foreseeable future. Frequently the same economic news citing lower employment shows gains in productivity. That's perfectly normal: Fewer people are making more stuff.

How could it be otherwise? The same manufacturing sector that produces the machinery — and computers — to help the farmers be more productive also makes productivity-enhancing equipment for itself. And, of course, the manufacturing sector has access to the wonderful array of tools we saw back in the first chapter:

Tools to increase reliability:	Total Quality Management
	Six Sigma
	Statistical Process Control
	ISO
	and others.
Tools to reduce waste and time:	Lean Manufacturing
	Agile Manufacturing
	Just-in-Time
	SMED (Set-up Reduction)
	and others.
Tools to enhance coordination:	Executive S&OP
	Enterprise Resource Planning
	Master Scheduling
	Kanban
	and others.

These are all superb tools. People in manufacturing enterprises are becoming better and better at using them intelligently and in learning how to use them in concert with one another. A sizeable portion of the productivity gains we hear about come from these items; it's definitely not all from factory automation.

We predict that the manufacturing sector will continue to decline in employment *but not in importance.* That's exactly what happened in agriculture. For the foreseeable future, manufacturing will continue to be a fine place to spend one's career, as it continues its transition from brawn to brains. And for those making a career in manufacturing, a tour of duty as either a full-time or part-time Master Scheduler will be very beneficial; it's a great spot from which to view the entire business, take notes, and learn.

The Future of Master Scheduling

On a somewhat narrower basis, much the same thing could be said about Master Scheduling: It will continue to decline in employment (the number of people working full time as Master Schedulers) *but not in importance.*

There'll be fewer full-time Master Schedulers in the future because as the manufacturing environment gets simpler, fewer people will be needed to control it and coordinate its various pieces. Lean Manufacturing and it predecessor, Just-in-Time, have enabled a dramatic simplification in the manufacturing environment, and that will continue. More simplicity, more speed.

In Figure EP-1, we can see this: As things become simpler and more reliable, less effort is needed.

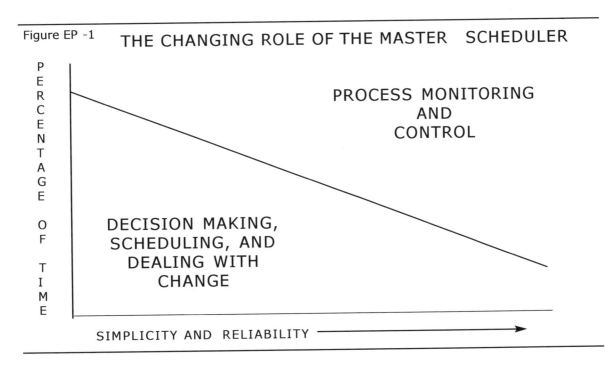

Figure EP -1   THE CHANGING ROLE OF THE MASTER   SCHEDULER

The Master Scheduling task changes as processes become simpler, quality improves, lead times shorten, Kanban is used more widely, mixed model scheduling takes hold, and so on. We saw this with Company K back in Chapter 8: Master Scheduling becomes less involved in making decisions about what to run and when, and focuses more on monitoring and controlling the processes involved in making the product.

We're already seeing jobs that once were completely involved with Master Scheduling broaden and expand to include some activities on the demand side of the business, such as customer contact, order promising, and the like. In other cases, the Master Scheduling function is being absorbed directly into the jobs of line manufacturing supervisors and managers[1]. These trends will continue and will accelerate.

Master Scheduling Principles

Regardless of how simple or complex the manufacturing environment, the basic principles of Master Scheduling apply. For your convenience, the principles we've articulated throughout this book are recapped in Figure EP-2. Feel free to photocopy it, if you like, and hang it in a visible spot.

We feel that these principles are the foundation for successful Master Scheduling, and that Master Schedulers who do their jobs in accordance with these principles will be doing their jobs properly and successfully. They apply equally whether you're doing Master Scheduling as one part of your overall job in a Lean Manufacturing environment, or if you're one of several full-time Master Schedulers in a more traditional and possibly complex environment.

Good luck and best wishes as we move ahead into the 21st century.

---

[1] What goes around comes around. Sixty years ago, the scheduling functions in manufacturing were largely done by foremen and superintendents as a collateral duty. That didn't work well at all, because the environment was so complex. The production control task, including Master Scheduling, evolved into a separate function, a necessary one given the complexity of manufacturing back then. Today we're going back to what we had sixty years ago: scheduling as a collateral duty. This time it'll work, because the environment is so much simpler.

Figure EP-2

Principles of Master Scheduling

M1. The Master Schedule must be managed to closely match the Operations Plan authorized by top management in the Executive S&OP process. (Discussed on page 9.)

M2. The Master Schedule must have visibility into all known demands, from both the external customers and also the internal customers. (p. 11)

M3. As the operational environment becomes leaner and simpler, the way in which Master Scheduling is used also should become simpler. (p. 19)

M4. Where practical, utilize the concept of Postponement: Hold off adding optional features into the product until after the customer order is received. Structure your products, your production processes, and your forecasting and scheduling processes to take advantage of postponement. (p. 27)

M5. Finish-to-order is the best order fulfillment strategy for most companies in most industries. It is more efficient and flexible than make-to-stock, and has shorter lead times than make-to-order. (p. 30)

M6. The Master Schedule must be under human control. The computer recommends; people decide. (p. 35)

M7. The due dates in the Master Schedule must be valid. They must accurately reflect when production orders will be completed and when customer orders will be shipped. (p. 43)

M8. Silence is approval. The Master Scheduler has every right to assume that products will be completed as scheduled, unless notified by Production or Purchasing that there will be a delay. (p. 45)

M9. Valid forecast consumption is essential for Master Scheduling to work properly. (p. 60)

M10. The Master Schedule can be the basis for customer order promising via its Available-to-Promise feature. (p. 72)

M11. You can't put ten pounds in a five pound bag. Effective Capacity Planning processes are necessary to ensure that supply is in balance with demand. (p.85)

M12. The Master Schedule and the Finishing Schedule are rarely the same thing. The Finishing Schedule is derived from the Master Schedule, and is focused on short-term supply. (p. 99)

M13. The Master Scheduler must see the true demand. When remote stocking points exist, their demand is dependent upon how those remote points will be replenished. (p. 115)

M14. Effectively dealing with change — in both demand and supply — is the essence of successful Master Scheduling. (p. 166)

M15 Master Scheduling is both a decision-making process (to balance demand and supply) and a communication proess (to solicit information and decisions, and to communicate the results of those decisions).

APPENDIXES

Appendix A
Executive S&OP

As we saw back in Chapter 1, Executive S&OP is one of the inputs that guides Master Scheduling on both the demand side and the supply side. Executive S&OP provides for demand and supply balance at the *volume* level, fifteen to eighteen months into the future. Master Scheduling, on the other hand, manages demand and supply balance inside the Planning Time Fence at the *mix* level, to the level specified by the Executive S&OP process. Both the detailed, item-level forecast and the Master Schedule must reconcile with the outputs of the Executive S&OP process.

The purpose of this appendix is to briefly explain how the Executive S&OP process works. For a full discussion of this topic, refer to Tom's earlier book, *Sales & Operations Planning: The How-To Handbook*. The new terminology in this area is discussed on page xv of this book.

The Executive S&OP process consists of five distinct steps shown in Figure A-1, below. Executive S&OP is done in product family groupings that are both forecastable on the demand side, and allow resources to be planned by the rough-cut planning techniques on the supply side.

In the figure we can see that the first two steps — Data Gathering and Demand Planning Phase — deal directly with forecasting. They include the tasks of: Data Gathering and Preparation,

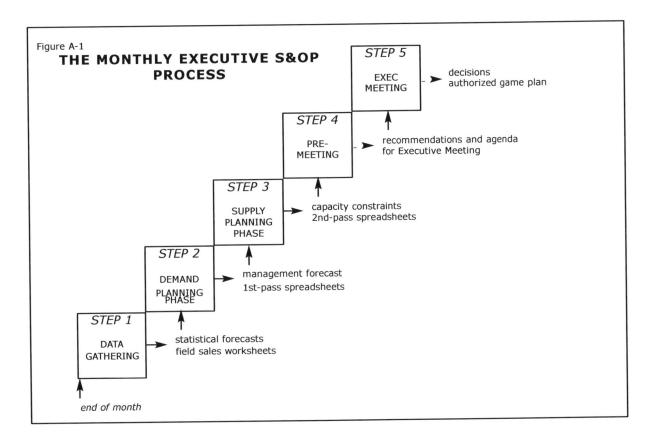

Figure A-1

THE MONTHLY EXECUTIVE S&OP PROCESS

STEP 5
EXEC MEETING
→ decisions
authorized game plan

STEP 4
PRE-MEETING
→ recommendations and agenda
for Executive Meeting

STEP 3
SUPPLY PLANNING PHASE
→ capacity constraints
2nd-pass spreadsheets

STEP 2
DEMAND PLANNING PHASE
→ management forecast
1st-pass spreadsheets

STEP 1
DATA GATHERING
→ statistical forecasts
field sales worksheets

end of month

Statistical Forecast Generation, Judgmental Adjustments, Documenting Assumptions, and Decision-making and Authorization.

From there, the monthly Executive S&OP process moves to a Supply Planning phase, which receives the authorized forecast from the Demand Planning phase and sets the initial balance between demand and supply at the volume level. Rough-Cut Capacity Planning is a technique that converts the forecast into units of capacity for the critical resource constraints. This conversion could be in hours of production, or rates of production on specific resources.

Next, at the Pre-meeting, key operating-level people make decisions within the framework of existing policy, strategy, and business plans. Also at this meeting, an agenda is prepared for the Executive Meeting, where higher level executives make decisions in cases where consensus cannot be achieved, or where actions recommended depart from existing policy, strategy, and/or business plans. The Executive Meeting attendance includes top management up to and including the president (general manager, CEO, managing director). Output from this session is the updated and authorized company-wide game plan. This in turn becomes the level to which the Master Schedule is planned on both the demand and the supply side, inside the Planning Time Fence.

Executive S&OP is an important part of managing a company's supply chain. Properly done, it is top management's handle on the business, dealing with all issues pertaining to demand and supply balance. It has the following characteristics:

- It helps people balance demand and supply at the volume level.
- It's a monthly process.
- It requires estimates of future demand, i.e., forecasts.
- It requires that supply be planned within known constraints.
- It operates in both units and dollars.
- It involves top management and key operating-level people.

Appendix B
Bibliography

APICS, *CPIM Participant Guide: Master Planning of Resources, Version 2.0,* Alexandria, VA: APICS, 2001.

APICS, *APICS Dictionary, 10th Edition,* Alexandria, VA: APICS, 2001.

Berry, William L., Thomas E. Vollmann, D. Clay Whybark, *Master Production Scheduling: Principles and Practice,* Alexandria, VA: APICS, 1983.

Brooks, Roger B., & Larry W. Wilson, *Inventory Record Accuracy: Unleashing the Power of Cycle Counting,* New York: John Wiley & Sons, 1995.

Clement, Jerry, Andy Coldrick, & John Sari, *Manufacturing Data Structures: Building Foundations for Excellence with Bills of Materials & Process Information,* Essex Junction, VT; Oliver Wight Limited Publication, Inc., 1992.

Cox, James F., & Michael S. Spencer, *The Constraints Management Handbook,* Boca Raton, FL: St. Lucie Press, 1998.

Davenport, Thomas H., *Mission Critical: Realizing the Promise of Enterprise Systems,* Boston, MA: Harvard Business School Press, Inc., 2000.

Goldman, Steven L., Roger N. Nagel, & Kenneth Preiss, *Agile Competitors and Virtual Organizations: Strategies for Enriching the Customer,* New York: Van Nostrand Reinhold, Inc., 1995.

Palmatier, George E., & Joseph S. Shull, *The Marketing Edge: The New Leadership Role of Sales & Marketing in Manufacturing,* Essex Junction, VT: Oliver Wight Publications, Inc., 1989.

Proud, John F., *Master Scheduling – A Practical Guide to Competitive Manufacturing,* New York: John Wiley & Sons, Inc., 1999.

Sandras, Jr., William A., *Just-In-Time: Making It Happen: Unleashing the Power of Continuous Improvement,* Essex Junction, VT; Oliver Wight Publications, Inc., 1989.

Shingo, Shigeo, *A Revolution in Manufacturing: The SMED System,* Portland, OR: Productivity Press, 1985.

Wallace, Thomas F., *Sales & Operations Planning: The How-To Handbook,* 2nd Edition Cincinnati, OH: T.F. Wallace & Company, 2004.

Wallace, Thomas F., & Michael H. Kremzar, *ERP: Making It Happen: The Implementers' Guide to Success with Enterprise Resource Planning,* New York: John Wiley & Sons, 2001.

Wallace, Thomas F., & Robert A. Stahl, *Sales Forecasting: A New Approach,* Cincinnati, OH: T.F. Wallace & Company, 2001.

Wight, Oliver W., *Production & Inventory Management in the Computer Age,* Boston, MA: CBI Publishing, 1974.

Womack, James P., & Daniel T. Jones, *Lean Thinking, Banish Waste & Create Wealth in Your Corporation,* New York: Schuster, 1996.

Appendix C
The Role of the Demand Manager[1]

Quite a few companies have created the function of Demand Manager. Depending on the size of the organization, this is sometimes a full-time activity, sometimes part-time, and sometimes requires more than one person. Here's a list of some of the duties that we see assigned to the demand management position:

• Assist Sales & Marketing management in sales forecasting.

• Coordinate the demand planning phase of the monthly Executive S&OP cycle.

• Participate in the supply planning phase of the monthly Executive S&OP cycle.

• Work closely with the Master Scheduler on demand and supply issues at the mix level.

• Coordinate decisions on product availability during periods of short supply.

• Help to resolve abnormal demand issues.

• Routinely reconcile the volume and mix versions of the forecast.

Frequently we see that the person charged with these kinds of demand management activities also has other responsibilities: serving as inside sales manager, heading up the customer service/order entry function, and/or performing other sales administration duties.

However it's organized, this is an important job. Steve Souza, a principal with the Oliver Wight group, says: "Many see the Demand Manager's job as a key managerial position in the Sales/Marketing organization . . . one highly respected by both the VP of Sales & Marketing and the president. Most often, they heed his or her advice."

---

[1] This material has been taken from *Sales Forecasting: A New Approach*, Cincinnati OH: T. F. Wallace & Co. 2002.

Appendix D
Order Quantity Rules

Techniques for calculating Order Quantities[1] are rules that govern the computer's creation of Master Schedule Orders (MPSs) outside the Planning Time Fence. The Projected Available Balance dropping below zero (or safety stock) tells the computer *when* to create an MPS; the Order Quantity Rules tell the computer *how much* to order[2].

In each of the following examples, the Planning Time Fence (PTF) is set at 4 weeks, the starting On-Hand Balance (OHB) is 65, and the Master Scheduler has set a firm MPS of 20 in Week #4. We'll see that the different Order Quantity rules lead the computer to create MPSs that are quite different in size.

One-for-One (sometimes called Discrete) tells the computer to order just what is needed to cover the net requirement in that week.

Product: #24680

Order Quantity = One-for One
Planning Time Fence @ Week 4

Week	Past Due	1	2	3	4	5	6	7	8
Sales Forecast		10	45	10	10	105	10	10	10
Projected Available Balance (OHB=65)		55	10	0	10	0	0	0	0
Master Production Schedule (MPS)					20F[3]	95	10	10	10

Explanation: The On-Hand Balance is consumed until Week 4, when the Master Scheduler has firmed an MPS of 20. This MPS satisfies the demand in Week 4, but is 95 short of the demand in Week 5. The computer then creates an MPS for 95 in that week, exactly equal to the demand, and does the same for each remaining week. This is the "purest" and "leanest" form of Order Quantity technique in that it facilitates driving the inventory to zero.

When Used: One-for-One order quantity is used when set-up (changeover) time is of little significance, and when there are no issues such as vat size, pallet size, etc. to impact order quantity determination.

---

[1] Sometimes referred to as Lot Sizes, Lot Sizing Rules.

[2] These same techniques also govern the creation of planned orders in Material Requirements Planning. However, in our examples, we'll discuss how the Order Quantity techniques apply only to Master Scheduled items.

[3] The "F" indicates that this order is a firm planned order under control of the Master Scheduler, not the computer.

One-for-One with Minimum puts a "floor" on the order quantity, telling the computer to order one-for-one, but never to plan for less than the minimum.

Product: #24680   Order Quantity = One-for One, Minimum of 20

Week	Past Due	1	2	3	4	5	6	7	8
Sales Forecast		10	45	10	10	105	10	10	10
Projected Available Balance (OHB=65)		55	10	0	10	0	10	0	10
Master Production Schedule (MPS)					20F	95	20		20

(PTF line falls between Week 4 and Week 5)

Explanation: The On-Hand Balance is consumed until Week 4, when the Master Scheduler has firmed an MPS of 20. This MPS satisfies the demand in Week 4, but is 95 short of the demand in Week 5, at which time the computer plans MPSs on a one-for-one basis, adjusted upward to the minimum of 20.

When Used: The minimum is seen most often in cases where it's not economical to produce less than a given quantity.

One-for-One with Multiple tells the computer to order one-for-one, but to always round the quantity up to a given number (or multiple thereof).

Product: #24680   Order Quantity = One-for One, Multiple of 20

Week	Past Due	1	2	3	4	5	6	7	8
Sales Forecast		10	45	10	10	105	10	10	10
Projected Available Balance (OHB=65)		55	10	0	10	5	15	5	15
Master Production Schedule (MPS)					20F	100	20		20

(PTF line falls between Week 4 and Week 5)

Explanation: The On-Hand Balance is consumed until Week 4, when the Master Scheduler has firmed an MPS of 20. This MPS satisfies the demand in Week 4, but is 95 short of the demand in Week 5, at which time the computer sees a net requirement of 95, checks that against the multiple of 20, and rounds the order quantity upward to 100 (the next even multiple of 20).

When Used: Vat size, pallet size, carton size, etc., suggest the use of the multiple modifier to the One-for-One Order Quantity.

Fixed Order Quantity tells the computer to always order the same, fixed quantity.

Product: #24680   Order Quantity = Fixed @ 100

Week	Past Due	1	2	3	4	PTF 5	6	7	8
Sales Forecast		10	45	10	10	105	10	10	10
Projected Available Balance (OHB=65)		55	10	0	10	5	95	85	75
Master Production Schedule (MPS)					20F	100	100		

Explanation: The On-Hand Balance is consumed until Week 4 where the Master Scheduler has firmed an MPS for 20. This MPS satisfies the demand in Week 4, but is 95 short of the demand in Week 5. An MPS for 100 is planned then, followed by another in Week 6.

Please note that the MPS in Week 4 is for 20. This seems to be a violation of the Order Quantity rule in place here, calling for 100. The key point is this: The MPS in Week 4 is under the control of the Master Scheduler. S/he can make the order quantity anything s/he wants. The Order Quantity Rules direct the computer; it can't deviate from them.

A side note: When the Fixed Order Quantity (FOQ) is insufficient to cover the net requirement, the logic of Master Scheduling tells the computer to order another FOQ's worth of the item. In this case, one might conclude that the FOQ acts like a multiple; it and One-For-One with Multiple seem to give the same result. There is, however, a subtle difference: The Fixed Order Quantity technique in many of the software packages will plan separate orders of one FOQ's worth each, in the same time period, rather than lumping them all into one larger quantity (as the multiple would do). This is helpful to companies who have clearly defined batch sizes and are hampered from making larger or smaller batches (the pharmaceutical industry comes to mind). At order release time, the scheduler is given an action message to release X batches of the Fixed Order Quantity — rather than one batch of a larger quantity.

When Used: This technique is used most often in situations where the company is trying to hit a balance between the costs of acquiring inventory (ordering costs, changeover costs, and so forth) versus the costs of maintaining inventory (capital costs, warehousing costs, and the like). The Economic Order Quantity (EOQ), a mathematical approach to balancing these costs, is one type of Fixed Order Quantity. With tongue in cheek, we point out that another type of Fixed Order Quantity is the use of an "NRN" (nice round number).

Other reasons to use the Fixed Order Quantity include establishing uniformity from one production run to another; container size (vat, tank, oven, and so forth), and in some cases, governmental regulations.

Period Order Quantity (Sometimes called Fixed Period) directs the computer to always order enough to cover a specified amount of time.

Product: #24680   Order Quantity = Fixed Period of 3 Weeks

Week	Past Due	1	2	3	4	5	6	7	8
						PTF			
Sales Forecast		10	45	10	10	105	10	10	10
Projected Available Balance (OHB=65)		55	10	0	10	20	10	0	10
Master Production Schedule (MPS)					20F	115			10

Explanation: The On-Hand Balance is consumed until Week 4 where an MPS for 20 has been firmed by the Master Scheduler. The MPS satisfies the demand in Week 4, but not the demand in Week 5. Guided by the Period Order Quantity (POQ), in Week 5 the computer creates an MPS for 115 to cover demand in Weeks 5 (95), 6 (10), and 7 (10). In Week 8, the computer creates an MPS for 10 to cover the demand for the balance of the horizon.

Please note: Minimums and multiples can be applied to the POQ as well as the One-for-One technique we saw earlier.

When Used: Period Order Quantity is often used for items that are cycled, i.e. run every so often. For example, if a cycled item is to be run once every six weeks, then a POQ of six weeks would be a good choice.

In Lean Manufacturing environments, the near-term Master Schedule is frequently expressed in days. Some products may be run every day, but others might best be run once per week. These latter items could carry a POQ of five, six, or seven days, depending on the work week.

Summary

Order Quantity rules direct the computer in the planning of MPSs outside of the Planning Time Fence. The Master Scheduler can override them any time s/he wishes.

MPSs, both inside and outside the PTF, drive material requirements and also requirements for capacity.

The selection of Order Quantity Rules and their specific numbers — for example, a Period Order Quantity of two weeks with a minimum of 50 — is a necessary part of making Master Scheduling work. However, these numbers don't need to be accurate to four decimal places; they need to be reasonable and "in the ballpark." This is *forgiving* data. Things like inventory records, bills of material, and the like are *unforgiving*; they must be highly accurate.

The techniques we've covered here are contained in almost all Master Scheduling software packages.

Appendix E
Safety Stock and Safety Time

Safety stock can be helpful in preventing stock-outs when applied properly. It is a hedge against uncertainty in demand or supply. In all cases, there are several cautions that need to be understood:

1. Safety stock must be applied sparingly or it will dilute the ability of people to answer the fundamental question, *What do I really need and when do I really need it?*

2. In many circumstances, there are effective alternatives to safety stock.

3. No matter how precise the calculations may appear, they only represent an approximation, based on the laws of statistical probability.

In many ways, safety stock is like a Trojan Horse — it appears to be a gift from a friend but can become the enemy if used improperly or without care. Be careful!

Uncertain Demand

There are two types of demand: dependent and independent. Dependent demand *depends* on scheduled production for a parent item, and most often affects components and materials. Independent demand typically is for finished products and thus is *independent* of schedules for other finished products.

Dependent demand should not be forecasted; rather it should be calculated from the upstream schedule for the parent. Independent demand must be forecasted, as there is no upstream schedule from which to calculate it. We'll confine our discussion here to items subject to independent demand, as those are most commonly encountered in Master Scheduling.

Since independent demand items are typically forecasted, they are subject to uncertainty and statistical variability. Safety stock, based on statistical probability, provides a level of inventory that will hedge against stock-outs when the unforeseen happens. The level of safety stock needed depends on the item's historical variability and the level of service desired.

Please note that the variability of the item, and not its total volume, is what determines necessary safety stock. To achieve a given level of service, a low volume item could require more safety stock than a higher volume item, because it has greater variability. An example of calculating an item's variability follows, using a technique known as Mean Absolute Deviation (MAD):

Period	Forecast	Actual	Deviation
1	10	8	-2
2	10	13	+3
3	10	9	-1
4	10	10	0
5	10	13	+3
6	10	9	-1
		Absolute Total	10
	Mean Absolute Deviation (MAD)		**1.67**

In other words, the average (mean) variability (deviation, forecast error) irrespective of whether that error was plus or minus (absolute) is 1.67. On average, the forecast of 10 per period is off by 1.67 units.

The second step is to determine the level of service that is desired. The level of safety stock required to achieve a given service level is based on the probability logic of the normal (bell shaped) curve. The following table of multiples is taken from that statistical information:

Service Level Desired	MAD Multiples
80%	1.05
90%	1.60
95%	2.06
97%	2.35
98%	2.56
99%	2.91
99.5%	3.20
99.8%	3.60
99.99%	5.00

With these two pieces of information, a statistical safety stock can be calculated, keeping in mind the result is an approximation. For example: If a 95 percent service level is desired, then a safety stock of 3.44 units (the 1.67 MAD times the 2.06 multiple for 95 percent) would provide for that level of service. If a 99 percent service level is desired, approximately 3 times the MAD (2.91 x 1.67 = 4.86 units of safety stock) would do the trick.

Once a level of safety stock is established, it would become part of the rules by which the computer would generate Master Schedule Orders (MPSs). To see how this works in practice, please refer back to Figure 3-3.

Safety Time as an Alternative

As can be seen in Figure 3-3, once a safety stock level is set, the computer plans to maintain at least that level of safety stock at *all* times. An alternative to this is to have the computer plan supply orders to arrive sooner than needed so that safety stock is only maintained when a demand is imminent. This approach is called safety time and works well for seasonal demand and also lumpy demand, or where the risk of obsolescence is high (such as in the fashion industry). For an example, please refer to Figure 3-4.

With safety time, the Master Scheduler could adjust the schedule as the sales forecast is consumed with known customer orders, removing uncertainty. This would be done with firm planned orders inside or outside the Planning Time Fence (PTF) and based upon the judgment of the Master Scheduler.

Benefits of safety time over safety stock include:

- Safety stock is carried for only the specified time before an uncertain demand.

- The size of safety stock is proportionate to demand and/or higher uncertainty.

- In batch production, it protects against whole batch loss or tardiness.

Uncertain Supply

There are two types of uncertain supply:

- That which is a percentage loss of planned production

- Loss of an entire batch, after completion

Percentage Loss

Percentage loss is also called shrinkage. It is the expected loss during the manufacturing cycle of an item. It is usually a percentage of the production volume, or it can be a fixed amount, based on destructive testing.

Although safety stock could be used to handle shrink, it would cause inventory to be carried all of the time, even when there were no open or planned orders causing the uncertainty. The best way to handle this situation is with a "shrinkage factor." It is assigned to an item and increases all open or planned orders by that percentage or amount. In this way, safety stock is carried only while the uncertainty of open orders exists.

Batch Loss

An unreliable manufacturing process that cannot be detected during production, but only after production is completed, can cause the loss of an entire batch. For example, suppose one in ten batches is lost after its completion. In this case, safety stock of a batch size would solve the problem, but would again cause the carrying of inventory, even when open or planned orders did not exist.

Safety time can be a more effective alternative. The safety time would be set at the time that it takes to produce a make-up batch. Keep in mind that a hedge for the necessary component parts and materials needs to be established to assure availability. This is one place where safety stock for a component would be appropriate. Thus, when a batch is lost, there is time to make another batch.

Additionally, the use of safety time is a good hedge against the uncertainty of the transportation industry, particularly for parts, materials, or products coming from overseas. Be careful using safety time for unreliable suppliers because it's only a matter of time until they know you're not telling them what you really need.

Conclusion

Safety stock is less important today than it used to be. Thanks to Lean Manufacturing, many industries have gotten very good at producing quickly, at the last possible moment. And thanks to the superb Total Quality tools we have today, production — both internally and from suppliers — is much more certain. A third important factor is some of the techniques discussed in the book — postponement, planning bills, finish-to-order, and so forth. Proper use of safety stock is important, but like all inventory, we should be working to eliminate the need.

Appendix F
Master Scheduling and Lean Manufacturing
by
Chris Gray
(cgray@grayresearch.com)

The purpose of this appendix is to introduce a number of the fundamental connections between Master Scheduling and Lean Manufacturing. These include:

- Scheduling at the pacemaker

- Pulling to the customer

- Supermarkets and buffering demand variability

- Mixed model scheduling and the EPE Interval

- Finishing schedules and Heijunka

Scheduling at the Pacemaker

One of the basic scheduling concepts of Lean Manufacturing is to schedule *at only one point* in the overall process, pulling work from earlier processes and flowing product to the customer through all downstream processes.

The point at which work is scheduled is called the *pacemaker*. The schedule at the pacemaker process controls the basic rate of production for a group of items with common process characteristics.

In a Lean Manufacturing environment, items that go through pacemakers are usually Master Scheduled. Although a basic objective of Lean Manufacturing is to produce only to customer orders, there are times when producing to a small stock, typically as a way to buffer the variability of customer demand, makes more sense than flexing labor and plant processes to day-to-day order variations. Consequently, in a Lean environment, Master Scheduled items may be produced to a finished goods buffer (a *"finished goods supermarket"* in Lean parlance[1]) or directly to a customer order. Items upstream of the pacemaker (components) are pulled from their source processes. Processes "downstream" of the pacemaker are handled on a first-in-first-out (FIFO) basis.

---

[1] Taiichi Ohno, considered to be the prime mover behind the development of the Toyota Production System, got some of his inspiration from observing replenishment processes in American supermarkets: When the bread shelf is starting to get empty, put more bread on it.

The basic rate of manufacturing and the basis for the Master Production Schedule is the *takt time* — sometimes called the "drumbeat" for the process. Takt time communicates the frequency of demand, and consequently the frequency at which a product must be produced in the pacemaker. The basic calculation of takt time is:

$$Takt\ time = operating\ time\ /\ required\ quantity$$

For example, if customers require 960 items per day and the factory operates 480 minutes per day, takt time is 30 seconds. To meet customer demand across all the products in the family, the Master Schedule must be set at the rate of one unit every 30 seconds.

An objective of Lean Manufacturing is to flow products through the pacemaker at the pace dictated by the takt time, and ultimately to flow those products through the entire process.

Pull to the Customer

The concept of *pull* is another essential idea of Lean Manufacturing.

Pull replenishment is based on a visual scheduling technique called Kanban. Inventory for an item is divided into equal units (Kanbans). As a Kanban worth of inventory is consumed it is reported, and when the inventory level reaches a predetermined level, a signal is generated to schedule replenishment. In a company with very short set up times, small order quantities, and lots of manufacturing flexibility, one Kanban of consumption might signal replenishment. In a company with longer set up times, several Kanban cards may have to accumulate before replenishment is triggered.

The visual signal used for Kanban could be a card, a flag, a ball, an empty box or tray, an empty rack or square on the floor, an empty truck, a fax, or an electronic signal.

Prerequisites for pull replenishment include:

*   Demand for the item must be relatively repetitive.

*   Lead times must be relatively short.

*   Components must be available so that an item can be produced "on demand" when the visual signal is generated.

For items that are being replenished using pull, traditional techniques often associated with MRP are shut off. Examples of what's shut off would include "order releasing based on planned orders" and traditional shop floor control based on push dispatching rules. However, executing to a pull signal is not in conflict with MRP planning itself. Typically, MRP planning continues to run for the purpose of projecting requirements for the plant and its suppliers of purchased parts and raw materials.

Ideally the Master Production Schedule (the "pacemaker" schedule in Lean) sends plans via MRP and the finishing schedule sends pull execution signals to the pacemaker process via Kanban, and this in turn may generate pull signals for component inventories.

Supermarkets and Buffering Demand Variability

One of Taiichi Ohno's innovations, the *supermarket*, provides an essential mechanism to Lean production, solving two specific problems:

- Provide a buffer of finished goods between highly variable customer demand and the pacemaker process that is often run at a more stable and leveled rate.

- Decouple processes that run at different rates — for example, a finishing process that flows at a constant rate and a process making components that runs large lot sizes at much faster cycle times but with significantly longer setups. A component supermarket might be located near the point of use, or near the source process, or it might not have an exact physical location, existing instead as a "virtual" buffer of circulating work-in-progress Kanbans.

Supermarkets in a Lean environment are significantly different from inventories in a non-lean operation. In a traditional environment, finished goods inventory levels are treated as a "guideline." However, supermarkets are sized and managed, and the quantity in the supermarket represents the *maximum* allowable inventory for the item. Consumption from the supermarket sends pull signals to replenish. Full supermarkets signal that the source process must stop producing. (In this regard, some people think of supermarkets as a group of Kanbans.)

Finished goods supermarkets help to solve the problem of demand variability in Master Scheduling. For many Master Schedulers, the biggest trap is the urge to "chase demand" — adjusting the schedule up one day because the demand is up, down the next day, up the following day, and so on. Although sensible forecast consumption is one step closer to not chasing demand, an effective Master Scheduler still has to use his or her best judgment in deciding whether to use safety stock and how soon to replenish it.

Although intellectually, most Master Schedulers understand the importance of schedule stability, often they cannot resist the urge to adjust the Master Schedule, even though there may be no real evidence of a sustained demand change in the marketplace.

In Lean make-to-stock, customer orders are typically filled from finished stock inventory buffers and those buffers are replenished quickly. Only what was actually shipped is replenished. Notice that this is a pull replenishment method based on actual consumption. It depends on both the idea of a finished goods supermarket for buffering demand and the ability to replenish the inventory quickly.

The finished goods inventory buffer, or supermarket, would be sized to meet the daily demand plus variability. Output from the pacemaker process would be set to meet the average daily demand. In other words, the Master Schedule would be set to bring in materials at the anticipated rate, while the finishing schedule (the daily execution) would be based on the actual mix of orders from the prior ship cycle or day.

The Master Schedule that supports the Lean make-to-stock strategy would have been created as a level schedule to show suppliers the daily quantities needed to support the drumbeat of the pacemaker process. What actually gets made (the finishing schedule) in the pacemaker process will be based on pulls from the customer (in effect replacing the inventory shipped from the finished goods buffer).

The Master Schedule is not changed as finishing schedules are executed — this is just another form of chasing demand and creating a volatile planning system. Generally speaking, the Master Schedule should remain unchanged until it has been demonstrated that the demand variability requires it to be changed. Without evidence to the contrary, the Master Schedule is doing its job — generating visibility to the suppliers for the daily requirements and the finishing schedule is doing its job — pulling material through the process to the actual customer needs, some days a little more than originally anticipated, some days a little less. Keeping the two in synch is the periodic releveling process that is used to update the Master Schedule based on evidence from the marketplace.

Of course, any inventory — even a managed finished goods supermarket — is waste. How companies will handle the variability of incoming demand and work toward the elimination of the supermarket will depend upon several factors:

- whether they can "level sell" to reduce demand variability,

- the amount of flexibility they have in the current process, and

- whether they are willing to use selective overtime to absorb demand variability.

A Lean company, therefore, can make the transition from make-to-stock to finish-to-order by slowly removing the finished goods supermarket and coupling the pacemaker finishing process to the shipping schedule.

In any case, the shipping schedule and the pulls from the pacemaker-driven set of operations must be leveled to feed relatively repetitive and constant demand to the plant and its suppliers. Otherwise the value-stream will degenerate into an uncoordinated, wasteful, disconnected series of processes.

Mixed Model Schedules and the EPE Interval

In a typical manufacturing environment, the biggest impediment to achieving a true mixed model Master Schedule is often setup or changeover time in the pacemaker process. Since the objective is to flow product through the pacemaker — ideally in a mixed model sequence — there needs to be a tool for determining the maximum frequency at which each item can be run without creating problems because of high setup times.

The essential tool for creating a mixed model schedule in a Lean Manufacturing environment is the "EPE Interval." The EPE Interval ("every part every interval") allows a company to determine the minimum interval — the time between runs — for every item going through the pacemaker. It answers the questions: Can we run every product every shift? Every day? Every other day? Once a week? By knowing the EPE Interval for the process, the Master Scheduler can establish an optimal mixed model schedule given the existing manufacturing environment.

In a company that's very proficient with Lean, it may be possible to run every product over the course of a shift. In less lean companies, the mixed model schedule might be to run every product once a week. Knowing the EPE Interval for the pacemaker process is the first step toward a true mixed model scheduling environment.

The Finishing Schedule and Heijunka

In a typical Lean Manufacturing environment, the finishing schedule is based on either pull replenishment signals generated at the finished goods supermarket or customer orders themselves. These pull signals are often communicated to the plant using a load-leveling technique, sometimes called the "Heijunka box," over a short horizon and in small time increments. The basic idea behind the Heijunka box is to distribute the finishing schedule evenly over time, typically in increments ranging from a few minutes to an hour or so, and in a mixed model sequence.

In many cases, the Heijunka process distributes the finishing schedule over the next shift or day, showing visually what is to be produced, when it should be produced (start and end time), and how much of each item is to be produced in each time interval.

The Heijunka mechanism is the principal visual technique for leveling the day or shift's volume at the pacemaker, and plays a key role in dampening demand. Through the use of supermarket strategies and Heijunka, the amplitude of highly variable, nonlinear customer demand can be reduced to levels that the plant can deal with.

Summary

In a Lean environment, the Master Schedule and the finishing schedule play an essential role in creating flow and level pull from upstream processes. To use Master Scheduling processes effectively in a Lean Manufacturing environment, a solid understanding of the elements discussed above is essential:

- Scheduling at only one point, the pacemaker

- Synchronizing production with anticipated demands using takt time

- Pulling to the customer

- EPE Intervals and the mixed model schedule

- Strategies for buffering demand variability, such as supermarkets and Heijunka boxes

In addition, you'll need to learn about other elements of Lean Manufacturing which are beyond the scope of this book. For more information on this increasingly important topic, we recommend James Womack and Daniel Jones' book, Lean Thinking, NY: Schuster, (1996).

Glossary

ABC Classification — The grouping of items based on their importance. "A" items are the most important; "Bs" are less so; and "C" items are the least important of all. This stratification can be applied to items in inventory, products, product families, customers, and more. ABC classification is based on Pareto's Law, the 20/80 rule, which states that 20 percent of the items in a group will have 80 percent of the impact.

Abnormal Demand — Demand not in the forecast, frequently from a customer with whom the company has not been doing business.

Accessory — A product that has benefit when used in conjunction with another product. For example, a docking station for a laptop computer is an accessory. Not to be confused with option; an automatic transmission for a car is an option. See: **Supply Item.**

Action Message — Output from a computer system that signals the need for action, typically with a recommendation as to what action should be taken.

Aggregate Forecast — See: **Volume Forecast.**

Assemble-to-Order — See: **Finish-to-Order.**

Available-to-Promise (ATP) — The uncommitted portion of a company's current inventory (On-Hand Balance) and future inventory, as expressed by the Master Production Schedule. ATP is an important tool in promising customer orders.

Bias — The amount of forecast error build-up over time, plus or minus. This is a measure of over-forecasting or under-forecasting. See: **Sum of Deviations.**

Bill of Resources — A listing of the important resources required to produce and deliver a given product or product family. Used in Rough-cut Capacity Planning.

Blow-down — The act of deriving detailed, mix forecasts from the aggregate, volume forecast. See: **Roll-up.**

Buffer — See: **Supermarket.**

Build-to-Order — Term popularized by Dell Computer which has a similar meaning to **Finish-to-Order** and **Assemble-to-Order.**

Business Plan — The financial plan for the business, extending out three to five fiscal years into the future. The first year of the plan is typically the annual budget and is expressed in substantial detail, the future years are less so.

Capable-to-Promise — An advanced form of **available-to-promise** (ATP). ATP looks at future production as specified by the master production schedule. Capable-to-promise goes further: It also looks at what could be produced, out of available material and capacity, even though not formally scheduled. This capability is sometimes found in advanced planning systems (APS).

Capacity Planning — The process of determining how much capacity will be required to produce in the future. Capacity planning can occur at an aggregate level (see **Rough-Cut Capacity Planning**) or at a detailed level. Tools employed for the latter include the traditional **Capacity Requirements Planning** process and the newer Finite Capacity Planning/Scheduling, which not only recognize specific overloads but make recommendations for overcoming them.

Capacity Requirements Planning (CRP) — The process of determining how much labor and/or machine resources are required to accomplish the tasks of production, and making plans to provide these resources. Open production orders as well as planned orders in the MRP system are input to CRP which translates these orders into hours of work by work center by time period. In earlier years, the computer portion of CRP was called infinite loading, a misnomer. This technique is used primarily in complex job shops.

Collaborative Planning, Forecasting, and Replenishment (CPFR) — A process involving participants in the supply chain centering on jointly managed planning and forecasting, with the goal of achieving very high efficiencies in replenishment. CPFR has been referred to as "second generation **Efficient Consumer Response**."

Critical Time Fence — See: **Planning Time Fence.**

Deferral — See: **Postponement.**

Demand Management — The functions of sales forecasting, customer order entry, customer order promising, determining distribution center requirements, interplant orders, and service and supply item requirements. **Available-to-promise** and **abnormal demand** control play a large role in effective Demand Management.

Demand Manager — A job function charged with coordinating the **Demand Management** process. Frequently the Demand Manager will operate the statistical forecasting system and work closely with other marketing and salespeople in the Demand Planning phase of Executive S&OP. Other activities for the Demand Manager might include making decisions regarding **abnormal demand**, working closely with the Master Scheduler on product availability issues, and being a key player in other aspects of the monthly **Executive S&OP** process. This may or may not be a full-time position.

Demand Plan — The forecast, customer orders, and other anticipated demands such as interplant, export, and samples. See: **Sales Plan.**

Demand Time Fence — That point in the future inside of which the unsold forecast is ignored in the **Master Schedule**. In many companies, the Demand Time Fence is set at or near the finishing lead time for the product. The logic is that the unsold forecast can't be produced due to insufficient time and thus should be ignored. See: **Planning Time Fence.**

Design-to-Order — An order fulfillment strategy that calls for detailed design of the product to begin after receipt of the customer order. This is frequently used in companies that make complex, highly-engineered, "one-of-a-kind" products. See: **Finish-to-Order, Make-to-Order, Make-to-Stock.**

Detailed Forecast — See: **Mix Forecast.**

Distribution Requirements Planning (DRP) — A technique that employs the logic of MRP to replenish inventories at remote locations such as distribution centers, consignment inventories, customer warehouses, and so forth. The planned orders created by DRP become input to the **Master Schedule**.

Efficient Consumer Response (ECR) — An approach in which the retailer, distributor, and supplier trading partners work closely together to eliminate excess costs from the supply chain, with the goal of enhancing the efficiency of product introductions, merchandising, promotions, and replenishment.

End Item — An individual finished product.

Enterprise Resource Planning (ERP) — An enterprise-wide set of management tools with the ability to link customers and suppliers into a complete supply chain, employing proven business processes for decision-making, and providing for high degrees of cross-functional coordination among Sales, Marketing, Manufacturing, Operations, Logistics, Purchasing, Finance, New Product Development, and Human Resources. It enables people to run their business with high levels of customer service and productivity, with simultaneously lower costs and inventories. It also provides the foundation for effective supply chain management and e-commerce. Enterprise Resource Planning is a direct outgrowth and extension of Manufacturing Resource Planning and, as such, includes all of those capabilities. ERP is more powerful than MRP II in that it: a) applies a single set of resource planning tools across the entire enterprise, b) provides real time (or near real time) integration of sales, operating, and financial data, and c) extends resource planning approaches to the extended supply chain of customers and suppliers.

EPE Interval — In **Lean Manufacturing**, this is the minimum time between production runs of each part produced in a process. (EPEI = Every Part Every Interval.) The EPEI calculation determines the maximum frequency at which each item can be run without creating problems because of the amount of setup time required.

Executive Meeting — The culminating step in the monthly **Executive S&OP** cycle. It is a decision-making meeting, attended by the president/general manager, his or her staff, and other key individuals.

Executive S&OP — The executive portion of the overall Sales & Operations Planning set of processes. Its mission is to balance demand and supply at the aggregate level and to align operational planning with financial planning. It is a cross-functional decision-making process involving the General Manager of the business and his or her staff, along with managers and other support people. Executive S&OP includes the functions of **Demand Planning, Supply Planning**, the **Pre-Meeting**, and the **Exec Meeting,** occurring on a monthly cycle and displaying information in both units and dollars. Used properly, Executive S&OP enables the company's managers to view the business holistically, provides them with a window into the future, and serves as the forum for discussing relevant policy and strategy. **See: Sales & Operations Planning**.

Family — See: **Product Family.**

Final Assembly Schedule (FAS) — See: **Finishing Schedule.**

Financial Interface — A process of tying financial information and operating information together. It is the process by which businesses are able to operate with one and only one set of numbers, rather than using data in operational functions that differ from that used in the financial side of the business.

Financial Planning — The process of developing dollarized projections for revenues, costs, cash flow, other asset changes, and so forth.

Finish-to-Order — An order fulfillment strategy where the customer order is completed shortly after receipt. The key components used in the finishing or final assembly process are planned and possibly stocked based on sales forecasts. Receipt of a customer order initiates the finishing of the customized product. This strategy is useful where a large number of end products, most often due to a high degree of optionality within the product, can be finished quickly from available components. Syn: **Assemble-to-Order, Build-to-Order**.

Finishing Schedule — The schedule that defines the operations required to complete the product from the level where its components are stocked (or Master Scheduled) to the end item level, assigns the resources (equipment, manpower) to be utilized, and specifies timing.
Forecast — See: **Sales Forecast.**

Forecast Consumption — The process of replacing uncertain future demand (the forecast) with known future demand (primarily customer orders).

Forecast Error — The amount that the forecast deviates from actual sales. Measures of forecast error include **Mean Absolute Deviation** (MAD) and **Sum of Deviations** (SOD). See: **Variability.**

Forecast Frequency — How often the forecast is fully reviewed and updated. A monthly frequency is common.

Forecast Horizon — The amount of time into the future that the forecast covers.

Forecast Interval — The size or "width" of the time period being forecasted. The most commonly used intervals are weekly or monthly.

Hedge — In two-level Master Scheduling, a quantity of stock used to protect against uncertainty in demand. The hedge is similar to safety stock, except that a hedge in this context has the dimension of timing as well as amount. Sometimes called the Rolling Mix Hedge.

Heijunka — A Japanese word that means "balancing." A Heijunka mechanism in **Lean Manufacturing** balances the amount of workload with the capacity to do it, normally in very small time increments. It also typically involves sequencing orders in a repetitive pattern.

Independent Demand — Demand for an item is considered independent when unrelated to the demand for other items. Demand for finished goods and service parts are examples of independent demand.

Just-in-Time — The forerunner of **Lean Manufacturing.**

Kanban — A method used in **Lean Manufacturing** in which consuming (downstream) operations pull from feeding (upstream) operations. Feeding operations are authorized to produce only after receiving a Kanban card (or other trigger) from the consuming operation. In Japanese, loosely translated it means card or signal. **Syn:** demand pull.

Lean Manufacturing — A powerful approach to production that emphasizes the minimization of the amount of all the resources (including time) used in the various activities of the enterprise. It involves identifying and eliminating non-value-adding activities in design, production, **Supply Chain Management**, and dealing with the customers.

Line Fill Rate — The percentage of order lines shipped on time and complete. See: **order fill rate.**

Load Profile — See: **Bill of Resources**

Make-to-Order — An order fulfillment strategy where the product is made after receipt of a customer's order. The final product is usually a combination of standard items and items custom designed to meet the requirements called out in the customer order. See: **Design-to-Order, Finish-to-Order, Make-to-Stock.**

Make-to-Stock — An order fulfillment strategy where products are finished before receipt of customer orders. Customer orders are typically filled from existing finished goods inventory. See: **Design-to-Order, Finish-to-Order, Make-to-Order.**

Manufacturing Resource Planning (MRP II) — See: **Enterprise Resource Planning.**

Master Production Schedule (MPS) — Future scheduled production, as represented by the (normally) bottom row on the **Master Schedule** display. These are the production orders from which customer orders are promised and which the plant(s) will be expected to produce.

Master Schedule — The tool that balances demand and supply at the product level, as opposed to **Executive S&OP**, which balances demand and supply at the aggregated *product family* level. It is the source of customer order promising, via its **Available-to-Promise** capability, and contains the anticipated build schedule for the plant(s) in the form of the **Master Production Schedule.**

Master Scheduling Policy — A document authorized by top management that defines roles and responsibilities. It directs the Master Scheduler and others on both the demand and supply sides of the business regarding who owes what to whom. It spells out who is empowered to make decisions under what circumstances and in which time zones.

Material Requirements Planning (MRP) — The first step in the evolution of ERP. This set of techniques uses bills of material, inventory data, and the **Master Production Schedule** to calculate requirements for materials. It makes recommendations to release replenishment orders. Further, since it is time phased, it makes recommendations to reschedule open orders when due dates and need dates are not in phase. Originally seen as merely a better way to order inventory, today it is thought of primarily as a priority planning technique (i.e., a method for establishing and maintaining valid due dates on orders). See: **Manufacturing Resource Planning, Enterprise Resource Planning.**

Mean Absolute Deviation (MAD) — A measure of forecast error. It refers to the amount that actual demand deviates from the mean (the forecast) on an absolute basis, i.e., irrespective of whether the error is plus or minus.

Mix — The details. Individual products, customer orders, pieces of equipment, as opposed to aggregate groupings. See: **Volume.**

Mix Forecast — A forecast by individual products. Sometimes called the detailed forecast. It is used for short-term scheduling for plants and suppliers, (and may be required for certain long lead time, unique purchased items).

Mixed Model Scheduling — A production and scheduling approach that interleaves different products within the same production line up. The opposite of "batch build," i.e., building all of the same product together, the mixed model approach runs different products one after another through the same resource. Advantages include better customer service, lower finished inventories, and higher schedule stability for suppliers.

On-Hand Balance — The amount physically in stock, irrespective of booked customer orders.

Operations Plan — See: **Production Plan.**

Order Fill Rate — The percentage of customer orders shipped on time and complete as opposed to the total number of orders. Order fill is a more stringent measure of customer delivery performance than line fill. For example, if only one item out of twenty on a customer order is unavailable, then that order counts for zero in the order fill calculation. The line fill percentage in this example would be 95 percent. See: **Line Fill Rate.**

Pacemaker — The point at which work is scheduled in a **Lean Manufacturing** environment. Components produced upstream of the pacemaker are pulled to the pacemaker finishing schedule. Work flows to processes downstream of the pacemaker on a first-in-first-out basis.

Planning Bill of Material — An artificial grouping of items in a bill-of-material format used to facilitate forecasting and Master Scheduling.

Planning Time Fence (PTF) — 1) The point in time inside of which detailed planning must be present in the **Master**

Schedule. Normally, the Planning Time Fence approximates the cumulative lead time of the product plus 25 to 50 percent. Sometimes called the Critical Time Fence. Most Master Scheduling software will not alter the **Master Production Schedule** within the PTF, only outside of it.

Plant Scheduling — The process of creating the detailed schedules needed by the plant(s). Plant schedules can include the **finishing schedules**, fabrication schedules, and so forth.

Postponement — An approach that calls for not adding the options into the product until after the customer order is received and then finishing the product very quickly.

Pre-Meeting — The preliminary session prior to the **Executive Meeting**. In it, key people from Sales & Marketing, Operations, Finance, and New Product Development come together to develop the recommendations to be made at the **Executive Meeting**.

Product Family — The basic planning element for **Executive S&OP**, where the focus is on families and subfamilies (volume), not individual items (mix).

Product Subfamily — A planning element sometimes used in Executive S&OP that provides a more detailed view than product families, but not at the extreme detail of individual products. Product Family A, for example, might contain three subfamilies — A1, A2, A3 — and each of those might contain a dozen or so individual products. See: **Product Family.**

Production Forecast — A forecast of demand for a module or option in a **finish-to-order** environment. Since this demand is of the dependent variety, it is calculated via explosion of the parent's **available-to-promise**.

Production Plan — The agreed-upon rates and volumes of production or procurement to support the **Sales Plan (Demand Plan, Sales Forecast)** and to reach the inventory or order backlog targets. The Production Plan, upon authorization at the **Executive S&OP meeting**, becomes the "marching orders" for the Master Scheduler, who must set the **Master Production Schedule** in congruence with the Production Plan. Syn: **Operations Plan.**

Projected Available Balance — The inventory balance projected out into the future. It is the running sum of on-hand inventory, minus requirements, plus scheduled receipts and (usually) planned orders.

Pull — The process of flowing production from upstream (feeder) processes to downstream (finishing) processes in which nothing is produced by the feeder until the downstream "customer" signals a need.

Resource Planning — A generalized term applied to **Manufacturing Resource Planning, Business Resource Planning,** and **Enterprise Resource Planning.**

Resource Requirements Planning — See: **Rough-Cut Capacity Planning.**

Roll-up — The act of creating an aggregate, **volume forecast** by summing up the detailed, **mix forecasts.** See: **Blow-down.**

Rough-Cut Capacity Planning — The process by which the **Operations Plan** or the **Master Production Schedule** can be converted into future capacity requirements. Frequently the Operations Plan, expressed in units of product, is "translated" into standard hours of work (which is a common unit of measure for production operations). Rough-Cut Capacity Planning can be used at the departmental level, or for subsets of departments, down to individual pieces of equipment or specific skill levels for production associates. This process can also be carried out for suppliers, for warehouse space, and for non-production operations such as product design and drafting.

Rough-Cut Material Planning — The generation of future requirements for materials via calculating Rough-Cut Material Requirements from the **Master Schedule** for short- to medium-term requirements and from the **Operations Plan** for longer-term needs, thus bypassing **Material Requirements Planning**. This process is very similar to **Rough-Cut Capacity Planning**.

Running Sum of Forecast Error (RFSE) — See: **Sum of Deviations**.

Safety Stock — In general, a quantity of stock planned to be available to protect against fluctuations in demand and/or supply. (APICS)

Safety Time — A technique in MRP whereby material is planned to arrive ahead of the requirement date. This difference between the requirement date and the planned in stock date is safety time.

Sales & Operations Planning (S&OP) — A set of business processes — **Executive S&OP, Master Scheduling, Distribution Planning, Plant** and **Supplier Scheduling,** and so forth — that helps companies keep demand and supply in balance, align units and dollars, and link volume planning with detailed mix schedules and plans. It does that by first focusing on aggregate volumes — product families and groups — so that mix issues — individual products and customer orders — can be handled more readily. The **Executive S&OP** component of Sales & Operations Planning links the company's Strategic Plans and **Business Plan** to its detailed processes — the order entry, Master Scheduling, Plant Scheduling, and purchasing tools it uses to run the business on a week-to-week, day-to-day, and hour-to-hour basis. See: **Executive S&OP**.

Sales Forecast — A projection of estimated future demand.

Sales Plan — The details backing up the **Sales Forecast**. It represents Sales & Marketing management's commitment to take all reasonable steps necessary to achieve the forecasted level of actual customer orders.

Service Part — An item used in the repair or maintenance of equipment. Also called spares or repair parts.

SOD — See: **Sum of Deviations**.

Stockkeeping Unit (SKU) — An individual finished product. In the more rigorous use of the term, it refers to a specific, individual product in a given location. Thus, product #1234 at the Los Angeles warehouse is a different SKU from the same product at the Chicago warehouse.

Subfamily — See: **Product Subfamily**.

Suicide Quadrant — Forecasting in great detail far into the future.

Sum of Deviations (SOD) — The cumulative sum of forecast error, plus or minus, over time. As such, it is a measure of bias. Also called Running Sum of Forecast Error (RFSE).

Supermarket — Within **Lean Manufacturing**, this is a set amount of inventory (finished goods or work-in-process) that allows **pull** processes to function when demand is not totally linear.

Supplier Scheduling — A purchasing approach that provides suppliers with schedules rather than individual hard copy purchase orders. Normally a supplier scheduling system will include a contract and a daily or weekly schedule for each participating supplier extending for some time into the future Syn: **Vendor Scheduling**.

Supply Chain — The organizations and processes involved from the initial raw materials through manufacturing and distribution to the ultimate acquisition of the finished product by the end consumer.

Supply Chain Management — The planning, organizing, and controlling of supply chain activities.

Supply Item — An item that is consumed in the operation of a product. Printer cartridges are supply items. See: **Accessory**.

Supply Planning — The function of setting planned rates of production (both in-house and outsourced) to satisfy the **Demand Plan** and to meet inventory and order backlog targets. Frequently, **Rough-Cut Capacity Planning** is used to support this.

Takt Time — In **Lean Manufacturing**, takt time sets the basic rate of production. It communicates the frequency of demand and thus the frequency at which products must be produced at the **pacemaker**.

Time Fence — A point in the future that delineates one time zone from another.

Time Phasing — The process of expressing future demand and supply by time period.

Time Zones — Periods within which changes to the **Master Schedule** are managed in certain ways, reflecting the realities of the operating environment. For example, in many plants, achieving a 30 percent increase in output within three days might be impossible, within three months difficult and costly but attainable, and within three years very practical. Time zones need to reflect these realities.

Two-Level Master Scheduling — A Master Scheduling approach where an end product type or category (not a specific product) is Master Scheduled along with selected key options, features, attachments, and common parts.

Variability — In the larger sense, this is the amount that individual elements in a time series deviate from the average. In some cases, variability is random and inherent in the process being observed. In this book, we used variability to mean the average forecast error per period. See: **Forecast Error**.

Vendor Managed Inventories —— A process that places the replenishment decision-making in the hands of the supplier. It's the supplier's job to not let the customer run out of stock and to keep the inventories at the agreed-upon levels.

Volume — The big picture. Sales and production rates for aggregate groupings — product families, production departments, etc. — as opposed to individual products, customer orders, and work centers. See: **Mix**.

Volume Forecast — A forecast by product groupings such as families, classes, and so forth. Also called the aggregate forecast or the product group forecast, it is used for sales planning, for **capacity planning** at the plants and suppliers, and for financial analysis and projections.

Index

Made in the USA
Lexington, KY
28 November 2016